SWIMMING
WITH SHARKS IN
DARK WATER

Having Race and Working with Grace
in Corporate White America

ATHENE BRINSON

 www.trafford.com

North America & international
toll-free: 1 888 232 4444 (USA & Canada)
fax: 812 355 4082

To my mother who taught me how to be a warrior.
To my mentor, Joy Pecchia, who taught
me that all dreams are possible.
To my sister, Pam Adams, who taught me grace.

CONTENTS

INTRODUCTION

Y ou are probably sitting at your desk and thinking that it is the end of the world. It is not. I know you think that you are about to lose your job. You are talented, a woman of color, and thought that by being yourself and demonstrating those strong leadership skills, you would be embraced and admired for the value you brought to the corporation.

But when you walked in the office, you realized that you are more "of color" and less intelligent than you ever thought. More "of color"—that is how people in the office see you; and less intelligent—your value (as you see it) was never really recognized. And now you ask yourself why.

The reality is that we live in a world of color, and this world is never more prevalent than in corporate America. Here, the galvanized white male figure is revered, trusted, admired, and (ultimately) forgiven for acts and deeds perpetuated during their professional lives. You, on the other hand, are a mere footnote in the glossary of diversity statistics that is shared among companies to prove that they covet and support the talent and intelligence of people of color. But you know better.

My story is the baseline for this book: my mistakes and travels through corporate America, attempts to make my mark, to garner acceptance and, hey, even a little bit of fame, only to find out that I had either placed myself in the position of the "professional corporate maid" or worse; understanding that even diversity statistics are not relevant when it comes to performance.

I do not want you to make the mistakes I made. I do not want you to take twenty years to learn how to do it right. I want you to walk in the door knowing the game and understanding how to collect your just rewards. I want you to learn how to swim with sharks in dark water.

When I started, there was no one and nothing that I could read that spoke to my situation. The self-help books assumed that I was starting on a level playing field, where the filters of color and gender did not exist. According to the self-help books, with skills, drive, and intelligence, corporate America would recognize my potential and provide mentoring and support. Why? Because I had value. And yet when I walked in the door, the support and mentoring, advice that I expected, was not there. To make things worse, according to the rules that I had read, doing a good job, contributing to the bottom line, I would be recognized and rewarded. Only performance mattered. In a way, some component of the myth does ring true. Doing a good job is what kept me working those few extra weeks or even months. As long as I continued to work harder, longer, etc., I was appreciated. The appreciation was acknowledged by allowing me to keep my job, overworked and underpaid. Meanwhile, I trained white men who went on to be my bosses or entered leadership slots or were recognized with money or plaques.

I could tell you the story as to how when I was a top producer at a company, I was the only one on my team who did not receive stock options. I could tell you that I was assigned roles in various engagements that when the bonuses were handed out, I received the smallest, even though I had made (and was told I had made) major contributions.

The reality is that although when I walked into an office, I saw individuals, I had no idea that color was such a separation of value. You probably think that this conversation occurred in 1970 or before—it occurred in 2004, 2005, 2006, 2007, 2010, 2014, 2015, 2016; and it occurs today.

Individuals are not racist by intent; they are racist by culture, heritage, and education. If I were to ask anyone if they were a racist, they would immediately deny it as a possibility. They would espouse their wonderful humanitarian acts or friends of color that would support an embracement of diversity that would make us all proud. The truth, I have never met a racist who knew they were racist. Even when educated as to what they have done, they would go to their grave stating that under no circumstances should I ever consider them a racist.

Where does this leave you? Sitting at your desk, or perhaps packing your desk. This book is designed to tell you that it does not matter how many racists you meet in the office; you can still be successful. It does not matter how many people use you or abuse you in the office; you can still be successful.

The fault of my failure was not in the racist actions of the corporation but in my lack of knowledge as to how to strategically maneuver myself through the myriad of minefields that that were placed before me. I realized that although I had gone to good schools, had a good education and solid expertise, I had no knowledge as to how to manage the jungle of white corporate culture. I knew I was a woman of color, *but I had no idea how to be a successful woman of color.* This I had to learn on my own.

This book is designed to help you identify, cope, and achieve success in those corporate environments. It provides you with advice on how to "swim with sharks in dark water." This book will help you use your "Spidey senses" to trust your gut, to identify when you are working on a plantation, and how to cope until you can leave. Oh, by the way, I need to tell you that you do not have the power at any time on any day to fix the plantation without permanently damaging your career. The people who have fixed these issues have sacrificed their career, possibly their livelihood, to ensure that we do not experience what they did. They shall always be the nameless heroes of our generation. We will always be indebted to those individuals who spoke up and lost their livelihood as a result. You need to understand that making a difference has a cost, and those who have done this have paid dearly.

Chapter 1 – The Rules Of The Road Are Important. You Are To Follow Them No Matter What You Think Or What You Believe.

When I was a little girl, it was my mother who taught me what it meant to be black in America. She was always fighting to be considered equal, intelligent, and of value in a culture that did just the opposite. She was never seen on television marching with Dr. King, but she marched in my life in a way that gave me courage to continue to ensure that all individuals, regardless of color, were considered of value.

I remember one day in particular; we were going to the supermarket during the holidays, when parking spaces were scarce. After circling the parking lot for about twenty minutes, she found a car that was leaving and patiently waited for the space. Right when she was about to pull in, another car, at high speed, took the space.

As the driver was leaving, he turned to my mother and used the "n" word to remind her what place she stood, not only in parking, but also in society. My mother slowly opened the car door and walked up to the man. I was seven. I also left the car worried that my mother was going to get hurt and unsure of what to do. The driver stood there as my mother turned to me and said, "Go get my gun." I looked at her; we had no gun, no weapons. She said again, this time with the tone that meant business, "Go get my gun." I froze. But then she said, "No, instead of the gun, get the knife. As soon as the MF leaves, I am going to slash his tires. No, get both. First, get the gun, and in the glove compartment, get the knife."

By this time, the driver had stopped in his tracks. Even though the parking lot was full, the area was vacant of people, and it was just my mother, me, and the driver. I started toward the car, hoping to God I would find a gun and knife that I had never seen or even knew we had. The driver looked at my mother who stood there like a Greek goddess under the authority of Olympus. I had started walking toward the car. The man looked at my mother, returned to his car, and left the space. My mother parked. We never spoke of the incident, and I never asked about the imaginary gun or the knife. I did check the glove compartment, and nothing was there.

My mother was a brave soul, and she stood up and fought every single time she or one of the family experienced racism. She was on a mission: to rid racism from the face of the earth. She said that it was up to us to ensure that racism was stopped whenever it occurred and that it was our job to stand up and correct the situation and "train" the individual that their behavior would not be accepted. In her mind, there was no injustice too small. She was dedicated in form and function. She was my hero.

Although my mother was an inspiration, as I got older, I could not use her tactics in the office place. There were no parking spaces here, and I never heard the "n" word. Instead, I found myself suffering the slings and arrows of racism. I was at a terrible disadvantage because although my mother had been my hero, my superwoman, the tools that she used could not be used in the office. I had to learn a new skill, a new way of fighting. For many years, I was at a loss.

When I started working in white corporate America, I was smart but knew nothing. One day I asked the vice president why there were no black people in management. He just laughed and walked away.

This book has been written to help you maneuver the world of corporate America, specifically white corporate America. This is an environment run by rules that are not written on paper but shared through a common culture, the culture of white men. I can remember being in graduate school reading the seminal literature on business, and every single example of the great thinkers were white men. How is it possible, through all the brilliance in the world, the great thoughts and inventions done by so many of color, that an entire discipline of thought is limited to one race and one gender?

This book is designed to help you through the difficulties, to give you tips on how to walk around and survive the elements of corporate America that are meant to trip you up. This book will give you guidance on how to become a successful leader in this (white corporate) culture without selling out who you are in race and gender. It is designed to help you embrace who you are in a world that may not embrace the things you absolutely love about yourself. Think of this as a survival guide and much more. Think of this book as your guidebook to the place you wish to be in a land that was never designed to consider you king. Yes, I meant king.

If you respond by saying "I do not have the skill set" and "I am not good enough," let me take the time to set you straight. Many years ago, my younger brother wanted to be a doctor. He had just graduated from undergrad studies but had not mailed any applications to medical school. I asked him why. He looked at me and said, "I do not think I am smart enough." You see, for many years, when he went to school, several white teachers had discouraged him from going to college. They had never told him that he was brilliant, special, and should follow his passion. Instead, they questioned his drive and advised a secondary path, a path that supported the white level of comfort. I knew this, and I responded, "Why not? I know a lot of dumb doctors." He laughed and mailed his applications. He received full fellowships to several schools. I tell you this story to say that anyone with the drive, heart, focus, and tenacity can be a success in corporate America. All the things that make you unique can make you successful. You were probably not told this enough, if you were told at all.

You may think that it is not the responsibility of the education system to tell us we are brilliant or capable of achieving our dreams. Perhaps or perhaps not, but I will tell you as a person of color, the chances of you hearing that you are capable of anything is far less. When I was in graduate school, I was sitting in class, taking a course from one of the premier thinkers of the topic. Next to me was a white woman. In the middle of the lecture, she raised her hand and stated that she did not understand a single thing he was discussing or writing on the blackboard. She said this in front of the entire class. The professor stopped, turned around, and said, "Don't worry, you will." Do you understand that type of validation this woman received? In one second, she was allowed to be comfortable in a state of "unknowing." If I had raised my hand and made the statement, my entire existence in the program would have been questioned. What I am saying in this example is that brilliance is not required for success in corporate America. Being perfect is not required, and it is even permissible to be dumb and lost at times in corporate America and still succeed. We, as people of color, believe (as we should) that skills, intellect, commitment, and focus should be enough; but it is not. You need to understand that because you are of color, you need a unique set of skills to succeed.

The purpose of this book is to help you become successful in corporate America by having you understand that being of color is a characteristic that defines you. Even though you do not define it as a determinate of your value, others do. The reality of that statement appears almost contrary to the wonderful politically correct language that we hear every day in the office. Use this book as a survival guide to help you respond to those slights that are thrown at us every day simply because of the color of our skin. This book is designed to give you the information that I have acquired over the years. I am going to share with you how to swim with sharks in dark water.

This book is going to give you a set of rules based on the situation that you may find yourself. These are rules that I have developed over the years and shared on a regular basis with friends of color, particularly women. The mistake they make (regularly) is to change their mind when applying the rule. They will usually say, "Oh, he is not that bad. Do I really have to ignore him?" The problem is that as women, particularly women of color, we are taught to be nice. Heck, we have to be nice. When nice does not work, we become mad. What we have not been taught is that there is a very comfortable productive state between nice and mad. You do not have to be my mother, but you do have to properly react to racist incidents in the office. You need to develop professional skills in combating racism. For lack of a better term, let's call this *Skills for Swimming with Sharks (SSS)*.

Yes, we are not taught to have SSS, or we think that SSS means that we need to be sly or cunning, dishonest, egotistic, and not a team player. In reality, SSS is simply understanding the unwritten rules of the white corporate environment. SSS is designed to manage your behavior in certain situations. When our heart tells us that we should be kind and supportive, but if we really understood our role in the office, then we would know that we are not responsible for everyone's success or failure. To do, this you may need to go against all those nice and supportive instincts that you have been trained to use. You may need to establish a new set of skills.

Now let's talk about why you get so angry. You see, because you do not have the skill (SSS) of managing a situation at work, after being so nice and agreeable, you get mad. That is why management only sees you in two states: overly agreeable and mad.

It is for this reason that when you are given a rule in this book, you must follow it, against all the nice and agreeable training. You must take the rules seriously. This requires discipline. Whether you understand the rule or not, you need to follow it to the letter. In all honesty, I wish I could stand by your side and give you the support you need to trust the rule. Trust me, please, every single successful person I have ever met have rules that they live by, even when those rules are difficult. After applying the rules of this book, management will see you not as overly agreeable or mad, but as kind and firm—the perfect attitudes for leadership. This book will help you use the rules of the game to acquire the success you dream. If you cannot memorize the rules, use this book as a reference. The following chapters will explain my discoveries to develop these rules and why they work.

Chapter 2 – The Realization— Understanding That There Will Be Times In Your Life Where You Will Need To Acknowledge That You Are Working On A Plantation.

This is your first day in corporate America. You have achieved your educational goals, you made it through the interview, and you are now starting your first day. Everything looks good. You have one problem: you are black and female. As a result, your experiences in this organization are going to be a little different.

Many years ago, I was promoted to director of an organization that supported strategic planning for a particular business sector. In a way, I thought I had made it. I had the education, the international experience, and the drive to really make a difference. What I did not know was that I was not working for an organization; I was working on a plantation. For years prior to this job, I had worked for a medium-size company supporting international business development. I was known for my precision, dedication, insight into the customer's needs, and much more. In addition, I worked with the best—a team of individuals with which I could bounce ideas, learn, and not just work, but also grow. I found myself looking forward to going to work. The company was purchased by a large conglomerate, and the employees were absorbed as a component of the acquisition. Everyone I worked with and admired left, stating the company's culture was unattractive. I stayed, and where they saw issues, I saw opportunity. I saw opportunity in the size of the organization and my ability to make a difference. I did not see what they saw. Within six months, I would experience one of the worst moments in my career, all because I did not see that I had walked onto a plantation.

I was given a job as director of a business unit's corporate development. I had two people who had been assigned to me as a component of the division. The company had over one hundred thousand employees, with about 5 percent being senior management. In that senior management pool, less than .01 percent were individuals of color. In other words, I was the only minority in my division, and although there was a minority senior manager in finance, majority of minorities (particularly black women) were support staff. As a result, I was always the only minority in meetings, on conference calls, and traveling to the corporate offices. My naiveté in this regard was legendary.

You see, like most minorities, when I wake up in the morning, I do not see a black woman. I see me, with all my physical flaws, suit too tight, shoes not comfortable (God, I wish I could wear heels all day). When I walk into a meeting, I see individuals, not color, not size, not gender. This company changed all that. Now I know that every single company I work for has the propensity of turning into a plantation. It only takes one person in authority who feels that whites are superior to change the culture to diminish you. It only takes one day, one moment, one act; and you find yourself only seeing color, gender, size. One person, one act, one day.

I had a friend who told me that "racism occurs in companies that are broken, where the culture is flawed, where they no longer seek the best, where individuals have agendas that are personal." Racism is the dead canary in the mine. In other words, the organization's dysfunction (the gas) is so present that the result is that aberrant behavior is permitted and sometimes encouraged. Racism is the residual artifact that occurs when other elements of the company are broken. It is simply one of the many results of a sick corporate environment. It took me a long time to understand that when a corporate culture is flawed, it encourages behavior and actions as a result of this dysfunctionality, and racism is simply one of the behaviors.

Now here is the sad point—most corporations have at least one division or area that is sick, which means that every single organization has at any one time or another a pocket of racism. *Every single company has the ability to create a plantation.*

Three days after I accepted the job, an older white man came into my office and said that he would rather punch me in the face than take direction from a black woman. I stood there frozen, unable to react. Being the ignorant person that I was, I immediately walked into the vice president's office and told him that I had been threatened and what the individual had said. The next six months, I endured what, in essence, was a consistent campaign to make my life hell. I did not know, but my status as a director meant nothing. I had complained about a white man. I was dead wrong in my immature thinking that life was fair, that my dedication as an employee would mean something, and that politics, influence, and race had no meaning in this issue. Politics, influence, and race were the only factors. What he said, and whether it was right or wrong, was not the issue. Eventually, the issue was boiled down to liability, and in addition to being a person of color, I had an extra label—I was a liability. Over the next six months, the company did everything to get rid of me. Suddenly, I found myself swimming with sharks in dark water, and I was chum.

I think the low point came when I was on my way to work one day, and as I opened my front door, a truck was parked right outside my house. The company had decided that I would work from home from now on, and the truck had the boxes from my office, which had been packed, loaded, and delivered. I was now isolated. I needed help. Now you may ask why I did not go to a lawyer. But I did. I spoke to several, and all (yes, everyone) stated that this particular organization was super aggressive and we would be in court for years. Several lawyers just turned me down over the phone. This is an important fact as you will learn later in the book. Now I use and depend on lawyers, but I ask for a completely different type of service.

A friend mentioned that there was a black organization that sometimes would intervene with large corporations on behalf of individuals of color. I had absolutely nothing to lose, so I called the regional chapter and asked to speak to the director. Over the next couple of hours, I poured out my story, detail by detail. The director of the organization listened and said, "I will call the CEO and speak to him about this. Give me a few days." Within days, he called me back and stated the president of my group had been fired. He said that I had made a difference and the CEO had found several improprieties in how the division had been run. He did not go into detail and said he could not, but he did say that I had made a difference. Yes and no. First, remember that racism is the canary in the mine. The president was not fired because of what had happened to me or the incident. The short but fast investigation identified a few financial improprieties in how the president was running the division.

In reality, the review of the president probably started prior to my incident, but raising the awareness to the CEO was just another nail in an already constructed coffin. It is very important to understand that when you are faced with severe and threatening racism, it is indicative of a corporation that is in distress and, as a result, a culture that is truly dysfunctional. Individuals in this environment are permitted, and sometimes encouraged, to release their frustration pursuing personal agendas and issues. Racism is simply one of many ways that corporate organizations "act out."

When I went back to the office, I saw several black employees on the elevator. They were talking about their promotion, new offices, and changes in the division with the president gone. I had made a difference. I ask you, at what cost? Could I have handled this better? Absolutely, and this book gives you my experiences on how I learned how to not only avoid the plantation, but also change the behavior of nonminority individuals around me when I find myself on a plantation.

Chapter 3 - The New Paradigm— Destroying The Myth Of Racism

Before we move deeper into the book, there are few myths we need to debunk. In order for you to be successful in the corporate culture, you cannot label an obvious racial act as racism. I understand that we have been black all our lives and lived in this country for most of, if not all, our lives, but racism is an old word that no longer serves us any use in our society. We, as people of color, did not create racism, and unfortunately, we did not define it either. If we had defined the act (or term), it would not take so much effort to prove it. Believe me, if you and I had defined racism, life would be so easy. I would not be sitting in the company's human resource department having to prove that an older white man threatening to punch me was a racist. When I say that someone is a racist, I am required to prove that their "intent" was racist, that they woke up that morning with the "intent" to do something racist.

Whenever you talk about a person being racist, what you are doing is moving the attention from you (the victim) to the individual who is the problem. Once you do that, you lose the focus of the conversation, and instead of solving the problem, the organization comes together to protect the racist. The word *racist* implies that there is an intent behind the actions, and instead of focusing on the "action," the organization focuses on the "intent." Whenever you accuse someone in the office of being a racist, the organization will inevitably pull the person aside and ask, "Are you a racist?" And of course, the response is always no, which means that the burden of proof has now moved to you. Here is the interesting part: the proof is not based on the actions. Now you have to prove to the organization, your peers, that he or she is a racist. This is an impossible burden. For unless the person is wearing a sign that states "I am a racist," the proof is near impossible.

Now let's take another example. Let's say you are riding in an elevator and your boss tells you that you will never be a manager in this company because you are a black woman. You decide to take that complaint to the organization. Now here is the difference. The conversation would be "Are you sure he wasn't just stating a fact?" "I know John, and he has a lot of black friends. I find it hard to believe that he meant anything by it." Or, and this is the big one, "You must have misinterpreted that statement, and I'm sure he never said that or said it in a way that it could be interpreted as racist." You see, to the organization, a racist is a person who comes to work in a white sheet, carrying a cross with gasoline and matches. The organization defines racism as "deviant behavior," not the subtle cultural acceptance that they have come to rely on in making decisions, creating perceptions, and assessing a person's value.

Rule No. 1: Racists do not look like crazed zombies.
They are normal people you work with every day.

In racism complaints, you have to prove that the "intent" of the person who said or did the racist act is a racist. "Bob could never be a racist. They just adopted a daughter from China." Or "He volunteered to mentor underprivileged black kids last year." This term has been sold to us, and it means nothing. We never created this term, and its current legal and cultural definition does not help us in any way. It is designed to place us on the defensive, to place the burden of proof on us, to ensure that the ability to prove that a white individual is a racist is near impossible.

There is one great example of corporate racism that you may use if anyone does ask you to "correctly" define the term. In 1962, a number of commercials were released by Starkist Tuna and continued for over fifty years. Charlie the Tuna was doing everything to become a Starkist Tuna. No matter what Charlie did, what new skill he learned, or who he knew (that was one commercial), Starkist (the voice from above) would always say, "Sorry, Charlie, only the good-tasting tuna gets to be Starkist." The sad thing is that Charlie would keep trying, trying to be better, stronger, more skilled; and no matter what Charlie did, he could never make the cut. I felt it would be better for Charlie if Starkist just placed a note on the door that said, "No matter what you do, you will never to accepted by Starkist."

Another example happened to me when I was in my twenties. I was at a high-end department store in Atlanta, Georgia, buying cologne, standing at the perfume counter dressed in my professional suit, my hair perfect, makeup perfect, having all the signs that I am someone who should be there. By the way, as a sad note, in those days, if you went to a high-end department store, you dressed up. This assured that you might be waited on, and less security people would follow you. Anyway, while I was standing there, a black homeless man came into the store, holding his private parts. He asked the sales clerk if he could use the restroom. Instead of answering, the sales clerk turned to me and asked, "Is he with you?"

The reality is this: you have been black all your life, and you know when someone has an issue with individuals of color. You know when you are being placed at a "career disadvantage" because of your color. You know racism when you see it. You are a professional at identifying racism. Do not sit around and wait for verification. Do not test your theory. Do not approach the individual and ask the question, "Do you have a problem with blacks?" Trust your "Spidey sense."

Rule No. 2: If you think a person is a racist, they are.

Understand, that when you think a person is a racist, you are correct. *Do not ever have anyone tell you that you were wrong when you used the word* racist. Trust that your judgment is correct because it is. If anything, you have accepted much of the racism you experience as a part of living. It is true that racism can be institutional. Institutional racism refers to an organization that has adopted the belief that individuals of color are of "less value," and racism, as a rule, is an acceptable and possibly encouraged practice. These organizations, as I mentioned above, tend to have many systemic organizational issues, with racism and the practice of racism being a residual issue related to their dysfunction. Organizations such as these, you should never work for, and if you find yourself employed by a truly dysfunctional organization, your only option is to find another job. But until then, follow the practices in this book.

Rule No. 3: Know your racial tolerance level.

If you are going to tolerate racism, you need to understand your tolerance level. This is the level of racism that you consider acceptable. The reality for individuals of color is that you regularly experience some level of racism. It is very easy to tolerate the person at the coffee shop or your neighbor down the street. But at work, that requires a little understanding. Surprise, your racial tolerance level is not based on what you can take mentally, but rather how much pain you can experience financially. If you have enough money saved, and you are highly skilled that you can walk away from the job and without taking a breath, well, that is what we call the perfect level of racial tolerance. At this level, you will politely admonish anyone who exhibits racist tendencies at work. You will feel free to use your talents in a manner that is creative, expressive, and valuable. Your level of organizational fear from repercussions is minimal, and you find yourself very comfortable being you. *This is where we all want to be.* However, unless you realize the value of this position, you could lose it overnight. Financial well-being is the foundation to your level of tolerance. The ability to walk away is professionally powerful. It is the greatest professional power available to anyone at any time.

Permit me to give you an example. One year I had the fortune to have two consulting gigs. For both, I was doing wonderful work and truly enjoyed the ability to move from one assignment to another with ease. But I noticed something during this time, that I was really comfortable with my ability to react to racial statements immediately, without the angst and anger that I normally exhibited. I had a little more tolerance, and my ability to respond was calm, forceful, and designed to set boundaries. One day I was meeting with the vice president and receiving a commendation for supporting an audit. The vice president was commenting on my work but then added the statement "I wish you could work on your tone." Now you see, as a black woman, if I demonstrate any type of passion, directness, or corrected anyone, the follow-up statement is "Please watch your tone." A clear forceful tone coming from a black woman, are you kidding? That is like hearing nails on a chalkboard for some white men. However, my response to him was "Just pretend that I am a white man, and you'll be fine."

Where the heck did that statement come from? What gave me the courage to say that? Had I suddenly gone mad? The reality was it was because I was working two great jobs and only needed one to truly survive. It wasn't my education or years of experience; it was that I felt economically safe. I had achieved the position (at least for the moment) of economic viability. That had given me the comfort level to respond in a manner that was corrective without fear. I immediately went home and called all my girlfriends. They, of course, applauded.

Now to achieve this position, you need to be at the top of your game (skill wise) and have between twelve and eighteen months of savings. On the flip side, if you do not have anything saved, or if you are the sole provider of your family (I had no savings and was a single parent when I experienced the worst racial incident in my life), then you will have to do what I did: *Keep low and take the punches hard.* In other words, if you have nothing saved, then be prepared to be placed in an uncomfortable position at your job and experience the highest level of racism *because the more financially vulnerable you are, the more likely you are to experience the worst that racism has to offer.* The racist (for lack of a better term) can sense your level of tolerance or if you need to keep the job. They can easily identify how dependent you are on your job's income for survival. Most of the time it is because we have simply told them: "Why are you treating me this way? Don't you know I need this job?" They know how free (or enslaved) you are, and the definition of freedom is economics. Freedom equates to financial freedom.

Now I know you are saying, "What do I do in the meantime?" You have to realize that unless you have an understanding of your finances and have saved some money, you will always experience some form of racism on the job. And that is a fact. There are those rare moments of heroism when, regardless of your financial situation or how financially secure you are, you are willing to walk away from a job. I was in these situations, and I understand.

<u>Rule No. 4: If you are extremely valuable to the company and extremely vulnerable, you are the perfect target to become the "corporate maid."</u>

Valuable and vulnerable is a deadly combination. You are the prime candidate to experience "the corporate maid syndrome." Let's say you are extremely skilled in your job, but for some reason, you cannot leave. You need this job. In your mind, because of your skill, you are safe. After all, you provide exceptional value to the company. Shouldn't they appreciate you? Yes. But not in the way you think. You will not be fired, and there is a good chance that you will not be laid off.

A white man's desire to be the best, to apply his skills, and to add value is commendable, rewarded, and cherished by the company. If we do the same, we are relegated to being the "help." A corporate maid is when a company works a black woman to near death. They look at you as a near-free resource, an invisible asset that can be used at will, a great tool that can be employed until it breaks. Late hours, additional work (normally beyond your pay grade), with no additional compensation. Every now and then, they will throw you a few compliments and maybe a pat on the back. No different from a maid who does a good job on the bathrooms. You will not receive a raise, you will be asked to pick up the slack from other nonminority personnel, and you will leave the office when it is dark outside and arrive early.

Every mistake you make will be highlighted, remembered, and used against you when you raise your head seeking equal recognition. Every idea you have will be transferred to someone else. For a short time, you will consider this a great place to be, for this position does give (us) the opportunity to use our skills, stretch our knowledge, and (something you should never want to hear) "make a difference." Knowing that we are needed, particularly when we need the job, is a wonderful feeling. We, as women of color, can naturally gravitate to this position. But one day you will arrive at work and look at your desk and finally understand that you have become "the help." You will note that you have not been sufficiently rewarded for much of anything that you do, and you will ask yourself how you got in this position. I thought that if I did my best, contributed, made a difference, I would be rewarded. I learned the hard way that skill and contribution (for a woman of color) does not determine success. It is important that you understand that doing well is not enough. You need to understand that you must couple your talent and skills with the day-to-day ability to swim with sharks in dark water. You must have finely tuned SSS.

Chapter 4 – Poor Behavior Is Universal.

Now here is the real surprise. If I told you that white was not always white, and that even in the definition of white, not all whites are considered equal, you would probably say that I am out of my mind. The dark side of racism is that it is done to nearly everyone at any time. Maybe not at the level and intensity of individuals of color, but the principles are applied to all.

Rule No. 5: They do it to one another.

Early in my career, I was a systems analyst working on a large information technology outsourcing solution for a Fortune 50 utility company. The deal was valued at over $4 billion and required a team of engineers, integrators, analysts (for financial and business), as well as support from executive management. In all, there were over sixty people working on the solution and approximately twenty working on the presentation for the potential client. We were on the top floor of the company headquarters working all hours. Our average day was twelve to sixteen hours. It is important to note that of the sixty people on the team, I was the only minority. We had been working for about two weeks with a presentation due in a few days. The sales lead, a senior sales associate for the company, was responsible for the final client presentation.

The presentation was broken into several parts, with the senior sales associates requesting a photo from each lead for the presentation. I had just finished my presentation and provided my photo and went back to the hotel for a few hours of sleep. Around nine o'clock that evening, I returned for a late meeting. The lights in the executive conference room were off, and about fifteen people were doing a walk-through of the presentation. I walked in as to not to disturb the process and took a seat in the back. The lead sales person was walking through the slides. A picture of the lead person for the employee transition component of the contract came up on a slide. It was the introduction to a major component of the outsourcing process. Immediately, someone in the room said, "Do you think she is white?" "No, not quite," responded another. "She has too many dark features." The picture was of a very attractive white woman with dark hair. The discussion continued with a very keen analysis as to what makes up white and what does not. To say the least, I was surprised. I thought that the categorization was binary. In other words, you are either white or of color. I did not think for one minute that there were degrees of white. The discussion continued, with hair and skin comparisons, in detail as to what entitled a person be called white. I could not take it anymore, and I spoke. "I had no idea that there were degrees of white." Immediately, the room went quiet. I assumed they were trying to figure out how long I had been sitting in the back. There was a little mumbling, and they continued through the presentation, focusing on the outsourcing elements. It was never spoken of again. But I found it illuminating. Who knew?

Rule No. 6: 99 percent of white Americans do not know they are racists.

A few years ago, I was refinancing my house. I started working with the loan officer, and as we discussed the refinancing, I walked through my financial goals, selected the mortgage product, and started filling out the paperwork. I then locked in my rate. Now here is where it gets interesting.

Before I give you the rest of the story, we need to discuss racism just a little more. Earlier I had said that most white people think a racist person is easy to recognize, for they are the one carrying the sheet, cross, and gasoline. In reality, most racists do not even know that their actions are racist. Racism is so embedded in our culture that it is no longer a learned action; it is visceral. In other words, it is an automatic response. Let's say you were raised with all the stimuli, book, media, conversations, that defined success a certain way, a certain type, a certain culture. Let's say that when you thought of failure or fear, you saw a certain culture, a certain type, a certain speech. Now let's say you have two candidates in front of you, and one represents what you have been taught represents success, and the other, failure. Let's say the one that represents failure has the better resume. What would you think? No matter, you would choose the safe choice, the success choice.

Shall we prove the point! Let's pretend you have been stopped by a police officer for running a stop sign, and as the police officer is approaching your car, you hear God speaking to you. God says, "There is a police officer approaching your car. Just ask and I can make you a blond-haired white woman for twenty minutes." Would you say yes? In reality, if God spoke to me, I would ask him to make the police officer disappear, but run with me on this one. The bottom line is you know that racism is subconscious and that no matter what you do or say, your color, your size, your means of dress will determine the next twenty minutes of your life. We understand this, we accept this, and we act to mitigate the personal inherent risk we experience because of racism during these moments. And yet we walk into an office, and because the police officer is wearing a suit and goes by the name of Harry, we do not even think about the personal inherent risk we have in the office. We do not think about creating responses, actions, etc., that would mitigate the personal risk we have in the work place. And this is the unbelievable part: we are always surprised when we find ourselves experiencing racism. We are trained by our parents and friends to protect ourselves when we are approached by a police officer, but we are not trained to protect ourselves when Harry in a suit approaches our desk. Why not?

Rule No. 7: We must create strategies for being approached in the workplace, with the same dedication that we create strategies for being approached by a police officer.

Now let's go back to the refinancing of my house. The initial intake officer (the person who takes your information and decides whether you initial qualify enough to move to the next step of the process) was very efficient. She stated that the loan officer would contact me and assist the underwriter approving the loan.

Once the loan officer contacted me, I completed all the paperwork, and then it started to happen. Papers were dropped; items were lost. The strange thing was the loan officer would always apologize. "I don't know what happened, I remember requesting the appraisal last week, but she/he never called me back." "Oh my goodness, I forgot that the employment verification was still missing." "Darn, I never received the title." Well, my locked mortgage percentage rate was about to expire, and the rate had increased. "Do not worry," she said, "the rate will be extended." Now you are wondering, did I just have an incompetent loan officer? Why did I think this was racism? Unless this has happened to you, no matter what I say right now, you will always be able to argue that this was "probably" not racism. But one of the aspects of racism is not just no; it is also a slow debilitating no. You are denied a right not because of a direct no, but because of a clerical error, a lost paper, a misplaced application, a lost e-mail, no e-mail, or a notification that was never sent and never received.

Denial of an opportunity through these subdued processes are not always done with intent. It is the discomfort of the white person processing the application. Something in their mind states that a person of color should not live here, have that, or work here. We recognize it, not in the first instance, but in the continual so-called incompetence of the white person we are depending on to process our application (whether it is for a job, a home, or even a benefit (e.g., public services)). Suddenly, our application is lost, misplaced, etc.

I started to step in. Every time she said that she was missing something, I asked for the telephone number of the person or organization that provided the missing item. I called the title company, the homeowners association, the employment for verification. I managed to fix every single broken item within one hour. When I called the title company, the woman said, "I do not understand this at all. We do a lot of work with this bank, particularly this loan officer, and we have never had a problem. We must have faxed her the information at least twenty times."

My loan was approved, and the rate had increased. I will never know if she had applied for an extension. Another loan officer called me to deliver the final loan documents. When I saw the rate, I nearly lost it. Instead, I explained the problem, every lost piece of paper, every act of incompetence. She forwarded me to the loan manager, and I repeated the story. But I said this: "I have no problem paying the higher rate, but the day after closing, I will be filing a formal complaint." He said, "Thank you, we shall look forward to receiving the complaint." My response was "Oh, not to you. I will file it with the president of the bank and the federal organization that manages banks/credit unions."

The next day I received a formal apology from the bank. Apparently, the loan manager had reviewed every e-mail I had sent to the loan officer and every issue that she had expressed in her various e-mails. He stated that he agreed that my treatment was "irregular" and the original rate I had been approved for would be reinstated. It is important to note that not once through my discussions with the loan manager did I mention the word racism. The loan officer's actions spoke for themselves. Whether she was incompetent or racist was not important; the issue was I was being denied something because someone else thought I should not have it. Who cares why! But here is the real kicker. If I had used the word "racist," suddenly, her behavior would not be the issue. The issue would be me, and I would be asked to prove that what she did, her systemic lack of competency, was because of the fact that she deliberately sabotaged my loan. No matter what she did, unless she placed hateful racist speech in an e-mail, this intent, her intent, would be impossible to prove. I have learned through experience that the word "racism" has no meaning to the white individual who is the racist. Once the word is used, it is as if a protective net goes over the racist, and the total issue becomes the person of color. *As a person of color, if you use the word **racist**, you will be considered the one with the problem.*

Rule No. 8: Many times the racist does not even know that their behavior is racist.

One more note, and this is important, I do not think that the loan officer even knew why she was having so many problems completing this loan. I do not think she understood her own discomfort in working with a person of color. All she knew or understood, in my opinion, was she did not feel comfortable completing this application, but she did not know why. It is important for you to truly understand that many times the racist does not even know that their behavior is racist. You calling it out and identifying the behavior as racist does *not* bring them any clarity or self-awareness to this behavior. But whether they understand their behavior or not does not excuse their actions. In addition, they have the comfort of knowing that even if I identify their behavior as racist, once I use the word "racist," the burden of proof is on me. If they (the person of noncolor) have made decisions that cost me time, money, freedom of choice, etc., they can do this with absolute discretion. They know that it is nearly impossible for me to prove that they did; they did because they are "racists". So, why would I ever use the word "racist" to define any behavior?

Chapter 5 – Learning The Swimming-With-Sharks Skills (Sss)

Okay, now that we have set the ground rules, you understand the systemic nature of racism, and you understand that you are perfectly qualified to identify racism. Now we need to start formulating and learning strategies to combat racism in the office place. Thus, the next rule may scare you. *As of this moment, you will pledge never to use the word "racist" or the phrase "he/she is a racist" in the office.* (You may even decide never to use this phrase again anywhere.) You are going to use a new term, a term that has bite, a term that does not require you to prove the intent of the person. You are going to use the term "abuse" or "abusive." In other words, you never need to label the behavior, only focus on correcting the behavior. Here, no proof of intent is required. The only thing that the organization will review are the actions, and for this, you have proof. Why abuse?

Rule No. 9: Never use the terms "racist" and "racism" in a corporate office. They will get you nowhere.

About seven years ago, I was working for a think tank supporting large clients. Most of, if not all, the employees had PhDs, and with my PhD, I thought I would feel right at home. The fact that the professional staff was less than 4 percent minority was not unusual. Considering my past employment, this was progress in my mind. I had a boss who was young and had been working at the company for a few years. He made it quite clear that minorities did not fit the image of a senior analyst. Using the experience that I had acquired from my earlier racial issue, I corrected him, kindly confronted him, and, when appropriate, escalated. I thought I was doing pretty well in handling the issue, and although his focus on me was still strong, I had successfully managed to perform and gain a strong reputation despite his issues with individuals of color.

But then something unexpected happened. My daughter passed away, and I was devastated. And after the company provided leave benefits, I returned to work. It was here at this moment that he decided that my weakness could be his advantage (remember, racists strike when they think you are vulnerable). On my first day back at work, he had the human resource person come by to visit me. He told me he was concerned. I found out later that the boss I privately thought of as Horror Boy had told management that the death of my daughter had made me unfit to return to work, which is why he insisted I talk to the human resource manager the day I returned from leave (without telling me, of course). After the human resource person left, he asked to meet with me, and he told me that he would no longer take my complaints; that if I wanted to keep this job, I would recognize that he could say or do anything; and that my job was to accept his word as law. Now I know what you are saying, "He said, what?" If you are a minority person reading this book, there is a good chance that you have heard something similar to this in your career. You have had a manager take you in an office and, with no witnesses, read you the law of the land; that you are now formally and officially on a plantation and under no circumstances are you to consider at any time that you are equal to the nonminority working next to you. In other words, your corporate maid status is official.

After he left, I sat there and cried. Emotionally spent, I really did not know what to do. Little did I know at that moment that this was one of the best days of my life, that I would learn something valuable, that would protect me for the rest of my career. The next day I was at headquarters for a meeting and still contemplating my next move. Yes, I probably could have picked up the phone directly after the meeting, called Human Resources and cried out my case over the phone. But remember, my daughter had just passed away less than three weeks earlier and I was emotional spent. Besides, if you remember, I had marched into HR before, and the only result was I, not the perpetrator, had become the liability.

I was trying to determine my next move, deciding if I should quit. Should I just leave? After the meeting, I was sitting in a friend's office, and I told her what happened, and she said, "Under no circumstances is that acceptable. Let me call the vice president of human resources. She is a friend of mine. I will set up an appointment for you to see her." The appointment was scheduled for the next day. This is when I started thinking. I had been here before, and there was no gain, just pain. After my last experience, I thought this was the worst idea ever, but she insisted. I needed to be able to appeal to the vice president, that his behavior was not right, that it was cruel, that in its purest essence, it was abusive.

This was such an inspirational thought. Who in the world would do what he did within days of my daughter's death? Who would treat anyone like this? He may have done this because I am a woman of color, but the actual act, in its rawest sense, was abuse. That afternoon, for three hours, I met with the vice president. I walked her through my tenure working with this man, and the meeting with him within weeks of my daughter's death. Instead of framing the issue as a race issue, I framed it as an abusive act that should never, under any circumstances, at any time be tolerated. And I asked her, "Is this the type of behavior that a company has, if it prides itself as an organization that has a reputation for creating true intellectual leadership?" Here is the interesting part: She looked me in the eyes and said, "*No*. We will take care of him."

Rule No. 10: Take away the intent, the reasoning, for the action; and in its purity, racism is an act of inhumanity or abuse and should not be tolerated under any circumstances.

Holy heck! This was easy, seamless, and appropriate. By just removing the word "racism" from the discussion and simply focusing on the behavior of the individual, I had successfully made him accountable for his actions. I did not have to prove intent. It did not matter one bit if he liked, disliked, preferred, did not prefer, certain types of people. His actions spoke, only his actions. All this time I thought that I had to speak as a woman of color. I realize that in the corporate environment, the reason for the behavior should never be on the table. The corporation should be accountable for the behavior and the behavior alone. I had been trained by my family, friends, and institutions that it was my job to fight for the race—equality. And yes, this is true: every opportunity I have, I should be educating and correcting the racist, that all people have value. By using the word abuse, he became the liability, not me. Who knew?

"Okay," I said. "What is going to happen next?" He was pulled into the vice president's office and given remedial courses in management, and I received a letter stating that he had been corrected. Now you think that I celebrated? No, not yet. Remember, for every action, there is an equal reaction. He came back from his remedial training with one thought on his mind: killing my career. Apparently, I had a little more to learn. First, when dealing with a racist (using that word again), the situation cannot be fixed. My actions may have provided the best solution at the moment, but I was still working with a racist.

Rule No. 11: Once you have identified someone as racist, no matter what you do, they will always be racist. You will never be able to change their racist behavior.

The bottom line is that I was still working with a racist, and although his behavior may have been muted, he was still a racist. Three months later, I received my review. Since I had labeled him as a dysfunctional leader, my review was administered by the Vice President. I received an exceptional review with a substantial increase in salary. There was such a love fest that I probably should have filmed the moment because a year later, he was back. It was like a bad horror movie sequel. He was back, but the environment had changed. The company had lost key consulting contracts, and Mr. Horror Boy was back in full force. His division was one of the few divisions that had met their revenue goals. His relationship with the client is exceptional (if you call getting coffee and carrying the client's briefcase a relationship). Suddenly, he could do no wrong. His behavior was back, the vice president of Human Resources had retired, and the company's acceptance for such behavior had increased. In other words, unless I had pictures or film of him burning a cross on my lawn and dancing in a white sheet, there was little they were going to do. As mentioned earlier, when a company is not doing well, this is when dysfunctional behavior is tolerated, accepted, and at times encouraged.

Rule No. 12: Do not try, and it is not your responsibility to fix the person or the organization.

Now my next review was different. As you can imagine, they complained about everything. I escalated to the division manager. I asked if I received such a good review last year, why such a change this year. The division manager said that the review was written by

Horror Boy, and as long as he had a relationship with the client, he could do whatever he wanted to me. I was speechless. I repeated the words in my mind. I then went to the restroom and cried. As I was standing in the restroom, a woman of color came up to me, and we discussed my predicament. She suggested I see a lawyer. I took a deep breath and left. But then I thought, perhaps a lawyer would help, but I needed to be strategic. You see, I no longer wanted to fix the organization; I just wanted to leave. I Googled employment lawyers and called the first one that came up on employment law. Standing at the Metro station, I told him my issue. He asked me, "What do you want me to do?" I said (to my surprise), "I want you to help me resign." He said, "Okay. How soon can you get to my office?" See, as I mentioned earlier, lawyers are important when swimming with sharks in dark water, but not to sue, to leave.

Rule No. 13: Lawyers do much more than just sue people. Use them as advisors, and if you find a good one, keep them for life.

When I arrived at this office, I explained to him that I wanted to resign the right way, not out of anger, but to ensure that my references and future would not be jeopardized. I did not wish to become blacklisted by a vengeful boss. I told him that I did not want any money; I just wanted to leave. I then told him my history at the company and, particularly, my experiences with Horror Boy. He sat down and wrote the letter. Smiling, he turned to me and asked, "Where would you like the letter of resignation sent?" I replied, "The president."

The letter of resignation detailed my tenure with the company, the documented events, the ongoing issues with Horror Boy, and the expectations that I would receive fair treatment in references and support for future employment in the industry, and if at any time it was determined that the company had actions that were not positive in my regard, the lawyer would pursue legal action. He then sent the letter. It was sent on a Friday.

On Monday, I went into the office and happened to see the company's client. I told the client that I had resigned and enjoyed working with him and wished him the best on the program. Within one hour, I had a response from the company. The client had called them and demanded that they make a counteroffer because I was critical to the program. They responded by sending a letter to my lawyer wishing for me to reconsider and stating they would like to hire me as a consultant for an undetermined amount of time for an undetermined amount of money. They also stated that they wanted to resolve the matter quickly. I told the lawyer that please tell them no but wait an "undetermined amount of time." I then went home. The next day, another company that supported the same client called me and stated that the client has asked them to hire me as a consultant to maintain my presence on the project. Meanwhile, Horror Boy came by my desk and congratulated me on my new job. I replied, "I have no new job. I would rather be unemployed than work with you for another day." I could not believe I had said that. But you see, over the past year, I had saved enough money to take some time off. And with a clean slate, references (which was why I had hired the lawyer), I was sure that I could land something. More important, since the death of my daughter, I understood the importance of life, and working with an abusive boss was not on my bucket list. I was prepared to accept the consequences of saying goodbye to a job. I know that this is a very hard decision to understand, but I also know that if you are a woman of color reading this, you understand, and quietly, you applaud my bravery.

I had learned a few lessons. Racism happens to women of color often—very often. You fix one issue, and you will always have another. In reality, nothing is ever truly fixed. You will always be swimming with sharks in dark water, but learning to navigate these waters and surviving is critical. A week later, my job at the think tank had come to an end, on the same day my lawyer sent the response to the company and successfully negotiated (in writing) how my references would be handled. At the same time this was happening, I was signing a contract with the other company for more money. Who knew that taking the leap and leaving the plantation would be okay? Who knew that lawyers could add value beyond suing? Who knew that it is was possible to walk away? Who knew that I could swim with sharks in dark water and survive?

Rule No. 14: If you are abused in the office, you must tell someone, and keep telling someone until someone helps you.

I find Rule No. 14 the hardest thing to do. Since the incident with Horror Boy, I have experienced abuse every now and then, and I have to force myself to follow Rule No. 14. Experiencing racism is not a comfortable feeling. Most people do not walk around and talk about the incident. Ninety-nine percent of the time, we are so shocked as to what was said or done that we probably get on our phone and call family and friends. But to discuss it in the office, now that is difficult. In this area, you must be careful. You are not permitted to exaggerate. This is hard. There are two reasons that we tend to exaggerate: One, we are so used to not having people believe us or take us seriously when we identify racist behavior that we have become accustomed to adding words that express anger and hurt with the facts of the incident lagging far behind. Two, we are the victims of one thousand paper cuts.

Rule No. 15: Recognize that some of your anger is because of the many paper cuts you receive every single day.

The other day I was at the grocery store and found a checkout counter that had just opened. I was moving my basket into place when the cashier walked around me and motioned to the white woman behind me that she was next. I call these incidents paper cuts. They are small actions that devalue us every single day. This is the visceral racism that I spoke about earlier. I do not think that people who are not of color understand how many paper cuts we receive every single day. You know how painful a paper cut can be; even though they are small and non-life-threatening, they are painful. Try having one thousand at a time. Could you imagine how you would scream in pain when you experience a racist incident at work? By the time you decide to tell someone what happened to you today at work, you are angry and hurt, and you feel you must show this anger for anyone to pay attention and help you.

It is important that you understand that this anger and pain does not serve you any purpose at work. The managers in your company who may want to help you cannot heal the paper cuts. They cannot even understand your paper cuts. The issue you have had in the past where no one believed you does not apply. That incident at the bank or the supermarket is not germane to the issues you are having at work. When you discuss the issue, you are not claiming racism. You are only discussing an abusive act that occurred, this one abusive act, not the one thousand paper cuts you received. You do not need to discuss the intent of the person or what they were thinking or what you were thinking. You only need to describe the behavior, factually describe the behavior and the discomfort you felt because of the behavior. Keep it simple.

Let me give you an example that happened recently. I had a new boss, and he decided that because I was a female and black, that I probably add little value to the corporation. *Okay, you are probably saying, how do I know that? Let's go back and review Rule No. 2: If you think a person is racist, they are. Remember, I do not have to prove to you that they are a racist.* Anyway, I was sitting at my desk preparing for the monthly program review, and he said, "I have reviewed your program review, and you may find it difficult to prove that the work you do requires a full-time person. I do not think you do enough, so expect some feedback." What? Okay, after years of learning how to deal with racism, instead of going "off on him," I said thank you. I then called the vice president and said "Mr. Stupid Boy (my nickname for my new boss) just told me that I may have trouble justifying my position. I wanted to take a few moments and provide you with an overview of what I do and get your feedback as to whether you think this is enough to justify my position." I then waited for the response. "What the hell is wrong with him? Do not worry, I will talk to him . . . You just keep doing the great work that you do." Okay, I did not stop there. The next day I had a meeting with another leader and said, "I am a little worried about Stupid Boy. He said that my work did not warrant a full-time position." Then I waited. Same response. Finally, when working with another of the key leaders, I said it again, and then I waited. His response was "Well, that's a little drama going on." This is what I mean by telling someone. Keep telling until you feel you have fully documented the behavior.

Let's talk about the advice I have been given about documentation. I have been told that when working in a racist environment, keep a diary on all the actions, statements, etc., that you have experienced that are racist. *This is the most stupid idea ever.* This advice was created years ago, when the poor person of color was given the "full responsibility and job" to prove racism. You would write down everything that happened to you. I guess you hoped that someone says something that is so horrible so you can write it down, with the "dream" of running to a lawyer and suing (for that big payday). In the meantime, you are walking around with a little notebook experiencing racism. You are not fixing anything. Your personal well-being, your mental state, and your work environment have become a potential legal case. Who wants to live like that? Who wants to work like that? Who wants to spend the best most creative years of their life walking around hoping to witness a racial act so you can write it down?

You want to have skills in the workplace that permit you to thrive, grow, and, of course, become more successful. What skills are you learning sitting secretly at your desk writing down negative and derogatory conversations? This goes back to my original thought: we did not create the definition of racism. This sounds like something stupid some nonminority came up with to move the burden of proof to the victim. Who can live like that? This is ridiculous.

The goal of any good company is to create a viable work environment, not a group of minority spies running around experiencing racism and given the job of documenting. Could you imagine that training? *"Hello, and welcome to Company X's training on diversity. If you are a minority experiencing racism, please keep it to yourself until you have a sufficient number of documented incidents. You will know when you have a sufficient number because you will experience depression, your skill set will atrophy, and you will have the reputation of being easy to insult and bully. And when you are about to lose your job or your sanity, we encourage you to walk down to the U.S. Equal Employment Opportunity Commission, hire a lawyer, and then spend a few years of your life pursuing a complaint that we will place all our resources to squash. Meanwhile, because of your loss of skill, depression, and inability to receive a decent reference (from us), you will probably either not work or have to accept a lower-paying job. We hope you enjoy your employment here."*

The bottom line is that you must learn to speak up when the incident occurs in such a way that you are comfortable, that you are not reacting from the one thousand paper cuts, and that you will keep telling people about this incident until somebody helps you. You do not have to worry about people believing you because you do not need to prove intent. Just state the facts.

You are probably wondering why I did not use the world "truth." Truth is so subjective. Your truth and someone else's truth can be so different. Truth is based on perspective. I personally call these different animals in the jungle. The lion has a completely different outlook from the gazelle. The gazelle is never really comfortable, always looking for predictors. The experience of being hunted is real, and therefore, their perspective of the jungle is based on precaution, safety, and risk. The lion has a completely different perspective. Every now and then, he may have to fight another lion for dominance, but the level of fear, safety, and risk is far different from the gazelle's. As a result, they have two different truths. Individuals of color have a completely different truth from individuals without color. It is very important that you know this when you are telling people about the abuse. The facts are good to communicate; your truth, not so good. Save your truth until you are talking to another gazelle. This is your family and friends. They will nod in complete agreement, pat you on the back for surviving, and probably help you with the pain you experienced from the incident. The lion does not give a damn.

For this reason, you must practice and become comfortable stating the facts. He said, she did. It is important to remember that I did not say exaggerate or talk about your pain—just state the abuse. He said it, it was abusive, and he should own up to it. It was said in private, and now it is public.

Rule No. 16: You only have a short time to correct the abuse.

I was working on a very complex assignment that required research. I had a young man of color assigned to complete the research. He was very quiet and small in stature. I was also working with an older white woman who had already expressed her discomfort in working with people of color. However, she was so unrefined (I will let your imagination run with this one) that she thought her feelings about people of color was actually a compliment. One day she walked up to the young man and said, "You remind me of my dog. You are so faithful and friendly." I was standing there when she said it, so I tried to give her a moment to rethink the statement. But being the idiot that she was, she repeated the statement with an even a warmer, stronger conviction. I was surprised that she did not start scratching his ears and patting him on the head. I went back to my office.

About ten minutes later, he came to my office to complain about the statement. He said, "She just called me a dog." I looked at him and said, "When a person insults you, you have between sixty and one hundred twenty seconds to correct the statement. If you do not correct the individual in that time, and you correct it later, it changes from a correction to a complaint." His delay in reacting meant that he had missed an opportunity to correct the statement with little or no repercussions. After all, it was a perfect scenario; I was standing right there. He already had proof that the statement had been made. He could have strongly reacted, clearly stating that being compared to the family dog was *not* acceptable, and any further statements of this type could not be appreciated or accepted. Instead, he kept quiet.

The reality is that we are not trained on how to react to "racist" statements. Instead, we sit there in complete disbelief that the statement was made (at all), and by the time we react, we have missed a wonderful opportunity to correct an action that could change how the individual interacts with us in the future. In other words, we could train the racist. Yes, it is possible to create an environment where you have trained the noncolored individuals in the office that there is certain behavior that will not be tolerated that you find uncomfortable or insulting. But this is a unique skill acquired over time.

Rule No. 17: It is your job to train the racist— train them as to what you will and will not accept in terms of their behavior.

You do not need to curse the individual (remember the one thousand paper cuts) or stand and give the black power signal. You only need to say, "I find that statement offensive, and I am asking you not to make statements like that again. I am not a dog." That is all he had to say. You have the right to correct someone who is abusing you. You have the right to request that they stop. You have the right to call out individuals on their behavior, and finally, you have the right to request an environment that does not single out individuals of color for abuse.

Most corporate racism occurs in private, behind closed office doors. Most abuse occurs in private. Both create shame within the victim, and the shame causes us to hesitate in asking for help. The shame causes us to draw inward, become private, only tell close family and friends. We feel powerless. This is why it is so important that you learn how to talk about abuse in a manner that encourages other people to assist or help you. There is no shame in abuse.

Review the following statements and think about my worst day in the office. I went to the vice president and said that a person had made a racist statement and threatened me in the office. Suppose I had said, instead, that I had just been threatened and did not feel safe at work. Suppose I had left out the context, words, and feelings of racism. Perhaps the response from the organization may have been different. I think that he would have become the liability and not me. "He just threatened me—help." That is such a strong statement. Suddenly, the liability is shifted from me to him. I would not have had to provide intent.

Rule No. 18: If you decide to burn a cross in my yard, expect an audience.

It is very important that you establish a reputation as a person of color who will not tolerate abuse. You do this by speaking up—factually. You do this by telling people and keep telling people until the abuse stops. You do this by understanding that the only real freedom is that ability to leave, to understand that only you are responsible for your economic freedom. You do this by understanding that you may have to tolerate more than you want to if you need the job. Understand your tolerance and make the decision on how much you will take strategically. Never let the racist define what you will take or tolerate. You define your level of tolerance.

Now here is the wonderful surprise: The racist expects you to become emotional and cry. The real win is that you no longer feel the need to try to understand the behavior and you no longer accept the definition of racism. This is abuse. Whether the person is having a bad day or is a racist is not your concern. Your only focus is the behavior. You understand the more you expose the behavior, the less likely it is to happen again. You also understand that once a racist, always a racist. Once the racist knows that whatever they do will eventually become public, they will either think of new ways to abuse you or they will abuse someone else. Oh, I am so sorry, you thought they would stop—wrong.

One of my favorite movies is *Guess Who's Coming to Dinner*. Sidney Poitier plays this perfect doctor of color marrying a young white woman. The movie has a certain elegance with topical discussions on race. And as a younger person, I always admired the way that Sidney Poitier interfaced with the family of his fiancée. But now much older, I am always moved by this one line. This is when the character that Sidney Poitier plays turns to his father and says, "You think of yourself as a colored man, and I think of myself as a man."

One of the things that racism removes from us is our ability to think of ourselves as a person devoid of any characteristics but our humanity, the ability to touch all people regardless of their physical traits and the ability to add our personal contribution of kindness and value to the world. When you no longer feel the need to educate the racist that they are racist, when you hold people accountable for their inhuman and abusive behavior, when you learn to tell people when abuse has occurred, these actions, in my opinion, is part of being colorless. The ability to insist that you are treated as an individual of value is when you start to find the ability to truly exercise your humanity. What Sidney Poitier's character was saying to his father is "I am free from the subhuman characteristic of color, I am an individual of equal or greater value than anyone else, and I have the right to think and dream accordingly."

Chapter 6 – Learning How To Swim With Sharks In Dark Water

At the beginning of this book, I discussed my worst corporate day. I responded by working harder and trying to convince an organization that a white man threatening to punch me in the face was a racist, and this behavior should not be tolerated. I went through hell for six months. I then discussed how I learned that racism at the individual level does not exist. That racism is a concept that was designed to move the burden of proof to the victim.

Although you have the most experience in identifying racist behavior, the world is not designed to support you but to limit the power you have in every racist situation. From there, we went to my next major growth in understanding that racist behavior (at the individual level) is really abusive behavior. Individual to individual, within or outside the corporate world, behavior that is racist is in its essence "abusive" behavior.

But what I did not mention was abusive behavior requires a few additional actions. It is important for you to understand that your actions and behavior also set a tone in the office. So there are a few rules that you must also follow to swim successfully with sharks in dark water.

Rule No. 19: Your office is not your home. Please refrain from moving in, and if you do move in, it will be the last space you occupy.

I am always amazed when I walk by a woman of color's desk and it looks like someone has moved in for the rest of their life. There are pictures of family, their favorite Bible scriptures, trinkets from their favorite vacations, food, cups, extra cups for friends, and other personal supplies strategically placed on their desk. If you were to ask them why there is so much stuff on their desk, they would look at you with disbelief and ask you why it is so important. After all, it is *their* desk. Now let's go down the hall and look at the vice president's desk. There are usually a few well-framed photographs of their family and a wall full of awards and sometimes degrees or certifications. You cannot tell what religion they are or how many children they have unless you go behind the desk and review all the photographs. In other words, they have not moved in. They understand that this office belongs to the company, and they are merely temporary residents of this office. But more important, they understand that they are temporary residents because there is a bigger office that they have their eyes on, and they do not want anyone to think that they are at home here.

I once worked for a very politically savvy executive, who, because of political climate, had lost his corner window office and had been moved to a small internal office that was the size of a file room. When we had meetings, I had to sit on a very uncomfortable chair, look over a pile of boxes, and discuss the topic of the day. I finally said to him, "I hate this office. How do you work here?"

He laughed and said, "This is all by plan. I purposefully have not unpacked nor made this office look moved in because I do not plan to stay here long. I want everyone who comes here to understand that this is not my office but a temporary holding area." Three months later, I saw him moving back into his old corner office, picking out couches, and hanging his new white board. I entered his office and closed the door. He said, "Never move into an office that you do not want unless you expect to be there the rest of your career."

If you think that by making your office "homey" that you are simply making yourself comfortable, you are wrong. You are signaling to the rest of the company that you accept your current station (that includes title, salary, job description, etc.) as permanent, that you do not expect a raise in pay nor in stature. You are very happy where you are. You are, in essence, signaling to everyone that there is no need to consider you for any other position in the company. I have two pictures of my daughter on my desk, and every day, when I leave the office, I clean my desk. There are no papers or materials left on the desk. There is no reason for anyone to think that I am settled. In other words, I am available for future opportunities and advancements.

However, there is another issue that you need to be aware of and think about in terms of what you place on your desk. I am always amazed at the number of women of color that will place religious articles or political material on their desk. *An office is designed to be agnostic.* That does not mean that God is not in the environment; it is simply for your protection. Why? If the person next to you places a picture of a known white racist or a picture of gathering of a white racist group on their desk, you would immediately feel insulted and feel that this is inappropriate for the office (or anywhere). You cannot request that someone not communicate their personal affiliations, either religious or political, on their desk if you feel free to place similar (but in your mind acceptable) material on your desk. Your desk, PC, or any other equipment or space provided by the company is not yours. This space must be treated as neutral territory. A few simple family reminders are appropriate. Many reminders of your success, awards, degrees, certifications are encouraged. And finally, if you expect a raise in stature, you must never give the impression that your current physical space is permanent.

By the way, that savvy leader I worked for within two months had moved (again) into the highly desirable corner office (two side windows) overlooking one of the best views of the city.

Rule No. 20: You will meet and work with individuals who look like you, but that does not mean they are your friends.

As mentioned in Rule No. 7, we are aware of the dangers of being approached by a police officer. We are also aware that the color of the police officer does not matter in terms of how we mitigate the risk in the potential situation. We, individuals of color, understand that anyone can exhibit racist tendencies and commit racist actions. We are aware of the fact that our risk is because of the position (police officer), not the color of the individual. And yet in the office, we do not have the same understanding. Many times we will approach another woman of color expecting that they have the same perspective. They may, and they may not. But to make the assumption is wrong and at times literally places us at risk.

If you are the victim of a racist incident at the office, do not expect another person of color to come to your aid because of their color. No more than you would expect anyone to come to your aid. Do not feel the need to discuss your racial experiences with this person nor share your anger or other issues with this person simply because of their color. I have made friends in the office place, but I am very careful as to how much I share with them. Notice I did not say share information or gossip. So to truly understand, let's go back to the discussion of abuse. There is a difference between telling others about the abuse to bring it to light and stop the abuse and merely discussing the abuse as gossip. You must never, under any circumstances, discuss a racist act in the office. All discussions on abuse should be for the purpose to shed light and stop the abuse. If you discuss the abuse as gossip, you diminish your credibility, and you place at risk the person you are sharing the gossip. All communication on the abuse should be professional. Your reputation as an individual who does not tolerate certain behavior is more important than the emotional satisfaction of discussing the racist. Call your family, call your friends, speak to a stranger on the bus (if you need emotional support). The office is not designed to support your emotional well-being.

Rule No. 21: Leadership opportunities only exist in organizations that are not sick (dysfunctional).

One of the interesting facts of my life is how I moved (permanently) from being a corporate maid to a leadership role. I had to learn the next rule the hard way. It is near impossible to be placed in a leadership role in a dysfunctional organization. No matter how much you try, no matter how much value you bring, you will be very much like Charlie the Tuna—Starkist does not want you. I will also say that if you are a person of quality and credibility, you may not wish to be in a leadership role at a dysfunctional organization.

The organization where I experienced the worst racial incident of my life, as I have stated before, was highly dysfunctional. Success had very little to do with capability but more with the ability to follow the sick culture of the company. It is important to note that this organization lost the majority of its market share and was eventually sold. During its years of downturn, I saw behavior that you would probably think was preposterous. In the last years that I worked there, one of the unusual events that I experienced was the phantom employee. I worked in a group of analysts assigned to support large deals. We had a gentleman (white) in our team who had left the company because of a terminal illness. He was a nice-enough person, and I had enjoyed working with him. Our leadership (boss) regularly talked to him and decided that she would keep him on the payroll until he died. We, the team, was instructed to continue to invite him to meetings and pretend to give him work. She would take some of our work and apply his name for submission (financial models, etc.). This went on for a year. Now you may say that this was a very nice act. But the reality is that, in a company, fairness and integrity is paramount. The employee's fake reviews, raises, work effort are, in its essence, fraud. And we do not know if the manager was receiving a percentage, particularly since she was so vigilant to make his employment appear real. We never saw the phantom employee, but we were told when he had passed away and was no longer invited to meetings.

We lived with the fear of retribution if we said anything to anyone about the arrangement with the phantom employee. In the meantime, I was always supporting a high-level executive developing a risk product for the financial industry. I showed up for work one day to find out that he had been escorted out of the building. What I am trying to say is very important. I know you have dreams about being in a leadership position. After all, that is why you spent so much time in school, getting certifications, etc. But if you are experiencing racism on a regular basis, then you are in the wrong organization. You cannot succeed, no matter how much you try, if you are working in an organization where abuse is the norm because it is an indication of other sick corporate elements.

However, even if you are working in a wonderful organization, you still must understand the rules of the road if you are to be considered a leader. When I was working for a small organization, which was later acquired by a dysfunctional organization, I had one of the top three bosses of my life. (Yes, I have had three great bosses.) Jerry was the first. It takes two things to place you in a leadership position. The first thing is that you must be given the opportunity (a door opens), and the second thing is that you must recognize the opportunity and take it to the max. I know that you think you can create the opportunity, and in some manner, you are correct. Very few people are given the opportunity unless they have demonstrated the skill and persona to successfully address the opportunity.

Rule No. 22: If you work for a functional organization, the door will open, but you must know how to step through it to ensure success.

Well, I had worked for Jerry for about six months when he called me up and asked me to stop putting his name on the various reports submitted to the senior management. It was considered normal practice for analysts to submit final reports to the executive leadership team using the senior manager's name on the report. But Jerry called me up and respectfully asked that I stop the practice and use my name. He said my work was sterling and I should get credit. He opened the door. From then on, I knew that my work was going straight to the executive leadership team, and I made sure it was my best. So I was not surprised when I was given the most sensitive assignment I had ever had in my life. I was asked to fly out and review the performance of a subsidiary, which was kind of odd. I was an analyst, and the subsidiary was actually in another country and managed our subcontracting relationships (supply chain) for a particular service.

Of course, I accepted the assignment, and within a week, I was landing and being driven to the office. This particular subsidiary managed a very low-cost supply-chain component. Yet when I drove up to the office, the average car in the parking lot costs over $60,000. There were high-end vehicles. Also, as I walked around the office, it appeared that no one worked. I was greeted by a senior manager who started a very long dialogue on the philosophy of the office. After being there for about four hours, it came to me why I had been sent. There were absolutely no minorities (and I mean *none*) working at the subsidiary, and because I was a black woman, I appeared as absolutely no threat. I was treated like a tourist, and I was given access to financial models, notes, meeting minutes, etc. It was obvious, after reviewing some reports and looking at the financials, that the group was receiving kickbacks from the subcontractors. They had underestimated my skill set (financials), and in a few hours, I knew enough to be worried. But here is the real beauty of my assignment. The real test came. What to do with the information? I could have called Jerry up and, in a very "gossipy" format, talked to him about the extreme gall of the individuals I had met and what they were doing. I could have called my friends from my hotel room and talked to them about the weird stuff I had witnessed at the office. After all, this was ripe for communication of some kind. But I also knew that for every door that opens, there is responsibility, and this was not about me.

You see, I had experienced enough at dysfunctional organizations to know that the people who rise above the issue, the individuals who follow the rules of integrity and fact, are the individuals who make a difference. These are the individuals whom I admire. Leadership is not based on white culture or white corporate America. It derives its roots from the purest sense of humanity, the ability to do the right thing in a manner in which the fewest are hurt. It allows you to understand that correcting issues does not require fanfare, but the real value is being in the position to do the correction. In history, regardless of country, race, religion, we have studied great leaders who all have the same characteristics. We know what these characteristics are, and they are not based on white corporate America; they are universal. Understanding the true basis of leadership is understanding the truest sense of humanity. So when I realized what I had discovered, it was like a small death to me, and I found it hard to share the knowledge of the death with anyone.

I went back to the office and wrote my report. I called it my Kevorkian Report. I called Jerry and said, "I am sending you three copies of this report, and I am deleting all softcopies." It was marked confidential. I then FedExed the report for Jerry's signature and never mentioned it again. Neither did Jerry. Two weeks later, I was getting coffee in the office lounge area when a coworker walked in and told everyone that the staff at the foreign subsidiary had been walked out by security. I said nothing. Neither did Jerry. I worked for Jerry until the company was sold. We remained friends for many years.

When I was young, as a person of color, I had visions of white corporate American leadership as making deals on golf courses and having three-hour lunches. We saw films of back office mudslinging and nepotism, backslapping behavior, and less-than-fair practices. Yes, this behavior does exist. But the reality is that most of this behavior is dysfunctional and ripe for racism or personal preferences resident in decision-making that are less than rational or optimal. As a person of color, you have little chance of making it in a company that operates in this fashion, and the company has less of a chance of being viable for long. Success and leadership are based on you being able to take your intellect, education, and skill set and apply them in such a way that they are uniquely definable and add value to what you do. You are your own leader, and when a door opens, you bring those leadership skills to bear.

If you are working in a functional company, and you are applying your skills in a manner that provides value, a door will open. Your ability to walk through and capitalize on the opportunity is based on you and only you. You need to understand that once a door is opened, the only barrier you will ever have is your ability to understand the responsibility required to ensure your success. Opportunities, regardless of color, are precious gems and should be coveted and treated as such.

Rule No. 23: If you need a job, you can work anywhere. If you want a career, work only for a functional organization

When I had the worst day of my life in corporate America, I was working hard for a dysfunctional organization. I thought if I worked hard enough, I would succeed. In reality, there was absolutely nothing I could do to fix the organization or ensure my future. In dysfunctional organizations, leadership decisions are egocentric and based on self-interest and personal preferences. In every racist situation I have been unfortunate enough to experience, the individual racist has never seen me as anything but an individual they wanted to get rid of, or a corporate maid. Now here is the interesting point: In every single organization, there are racists, so how do you know if you are working for a functional organization? Before I answer that question, I need to give you advice that an old woman once gave me. I think I was sitting at a bus stop in my twenties, and we were discussing men. I wish I knew her name because the advice she gave me was invaluable. She said that if you are dating a man, and you have nothing new in your closet at least every three months, then drop the guy. She was saying that if you are dating someone who cares about you, they will continue to encourage you to invest in yourself. How you look and how you feel will be important, and they will encourage you to purchase something new for yourself on a regular basis. I love this advice.

So how do you know that you are working for a functional organization? The same way you know you are dating someone that is right for you—*doors will open on a regular basis.* If you are working for an organization and a door does not open within the first three months you are there, and you have experienced racism, you are in the wrong place. Start looking.

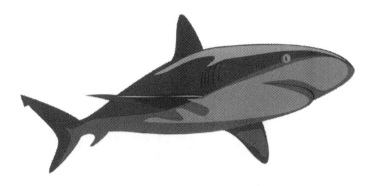

Chapter 7 – Racists Have Ways To Destroy You, And Many Of Them Are Surprisingly Creative

So after the worst racist incident of my life, I had little choice but to try to hang on to my job. I did not know enough to hire a lawyer to negotiate references, and I had not saved enough money to leave. In other words, my racial tolerance was nonexistent, and I was stuck. After the president was walked out of the office, I was given an assignment. I think the company thought that I would eventually quit, but they did not understand how much a woman of color can take when she has a family, is the sole provider, and really needs the job.

Little by little over time, I climbed back up from the career hell I was in by working extra hours and turning in great work. In other words, I volunteered to become the corporate maid, with the full understanding of what it meant. I started receiving international assignments and was sitting in a hotel in Europe when I received a call from a recruiter. The recruiter had a wonderful opportunity. After a few conversations, I was on a plane for my first interview. I was placed in a suite in a hotel and picked up by private car. The interview went well, and several months later, I had an executive package for relocation, a signing bonus, and a great salary.

Now I know you are thinking, *Girl, you finally made it.* But it was a setup. I was laid off within six months. Years later, I spoke to a few other women of color who had similar experiences. The final nail was when I went for an interview, a few years later, and the recruiter said to me, "You know you were set up." I remembered ten years earlier I worked for an executive who hated an employee. He felt the employee was a threat. He told me one day in a meeting that he had forwarded the employee's resume to a head hunter (with glowing reviews). A few months later, the employee was gone.

Over time, I have met many women of color who experienced the same setup. They were performing well in a company that had exhibited racist behavior, but because of their sterling performance, they were difficult to get rid of. Suddenly, they receive an offer they cannot turn down. A few months later, the job disappears, and they lose everything. You see, I was so miserable where I was and so hated that when the recruiter called, I thought I had finally been recognized for my value. I deluded myself to think that a recruiter had found me in a foreign hotel room and out of the blue would offer me the job of my dreams. In every single case that I have discovered, the job was either a client of the company they worked for or someone (an executive) who worked with the company or the recruiter.

<u>Rule No. 24: If you are working for a racist organization, be suspicious of success. There are so many ways to destroy you.</u>

The difference between this situation and the one concerning the executive is that for a white person, that goal is simply to get the person out of the company. For a person of color, the goal is to destroy your future. Moving you to another city (or country) and then laying you off less than one year later is perfect. However, in my case, it turned out to be a blessing. I had purchased a home in the country, on the water, and sold it for a premium. I also hired a lawyer to negotiate the exit package.

What did I learn from this situation? When you are working for a racist organization, you should be suspicious of any opportunity or offer. And this is very important. It was not the job offer that was the issue. The issue was that I signed the job offer without the advice of a lawyer, that I did not mitigate the risk by insisting on an exit package. If I had requested an exit package, one or two things would have occurred. First, if it were a setup, the offer would have been rescinded. Second, if it were a legitimate offer, the company would have understood my risk and honestly negotiated to mitigate my and their risk in the situation. As a woman of color, I thought the only time you hired a lawyer was to sue. In reality, they are used to keep you from making mistakes, as I noted in Rule No. 13. When you are working for a racist organization, do not underestimate their ability to seek to bring you to your knees.

Chapter 8 – Learning To Identify The Sharks You Swim With

When I first started this journey of understanding how to manage racism in white corporate America, I first had to recognize that my actions and reactions were also responsible for my success or failure. I could not control the racists' behavior, but I could control mine. More importantly, I could make an impact on the amount and level of racism by my ability to be proactive in the situations in the office place. When I experienced the worst racist event of my life, I did everything wrong. I followed a playbook that was not made to help the victim, but to support the racist. As I said earlier, we did not define racism, nor were we responsible for establishing the civil penalties. I had to develop a method of successfully navigating the white corporate environment; I had to learn to swim with sharks in dark water. But I had another vison: I wanted to do it with grace, not as the sad angry minority woman who is so often shown on television in reality shows. I wanted to empower myself to be me. I want to be able to work with grace in this environment where I am automatically culturally devalued the moment I walk in the door.

In this end, the most important rule that I created for myself was Rule No. 7. I wanted to create strategies for being approached in the workplace with the same dedication that I create strategies for being approached by a police officer. I also recognized that when we speak to our parents about what to do when a police officer approaches the car, there is usually one or two simple strategies. In the workplace, the environment is much subtler, in terms of danger, and much more complex. There are different types of racists, and each has a different racist behavior. I started to note the different behaviors and developed guidelines on how to combat it and protect myself. I started to understand that my behavior had to be much more proactive and much more aware of who and what I was dealing with.

Now there was a second problem. I like what I do, and I love contributing to a product or deliverable. I love being part of a team. I noted that many times my dedication to the product/deliverable was causing me to overlook the dynamics of the situation. I had to overcome my own faults and issues in terms of my continued need to view the office as a place of equality, when it is an environment of cultural dynamics spattered with individual issues and baggage that also need to be identified and managed. So I asked myself, how could I overcome my own lack of awareness within the culture of white corporate America? What could I do to incorporate discipline in my behavior? What strategies could I develop that would protect me, allow me to be me, and contribute to my success?

It was by accident that I found the answer. I started to assign nicknames to individuals. These nicknames would be cues to my behavior around this person. It worked. It worked so well that I had friends calling me from around the world describing an action or behavior of their boss or peer and me providing guidance as to how to manage the person or respond to the situation. Using nicknames removes the automatic response, the natural human response. Most of us are kind, supportive people, but if the individual you are dealing with is a racist, you cannot—you must not—follow the behavior you would use for someone you respect or care about. These individuals are different, and they must be treated with the full understanding that they place you in a vulnerable position. You know and understand this when a policeman approaches your car, and your behavior becomes controlled and based on actions that you have been told are successful in such situations where you need protection. When you identify a racist in the office, the same protective behavior must be applied.

The second need for nicknames was the full understanding that there are different types of racist, as discussed earlier. Some are aggressive, some are passive, some are cruel, some are confronting, and some are covert. You cannot use the same protective behavior with each one. With my over twenty years of working in white corporate America, I eventually identified a few major racist archetypes (sharks). It is these sharks that are discussed in this chapter.

This chapter walks through the major sharks. From my experience, the majority of sharks fall into these categories, although there are always a few rare species swimming around. You may also find at times that a shark has combined characteristics of several sharks (this is rare). Below is an overview of each shark with basic characteristics and guidelines on what I have found is the best way to manage each one.

There is one basic element to this information: you *must* follow the guidelines on how to deal with each shark throughout your tenure or for as long as you must deal or work with each one. The guidelines work, and because they work, your environment will be better. Sometimes because we have minimized the impact of the behavior through the guidelines, we relax. Please do not do this.

Once you have identified a particular type of shark, your behavior must be consistent throughout your relationship. The reason the individual is easier to work with is not because they have become nicer; it is because your behavior has mitigated the damage or harm they could cause, just as your behavior minimizes the impact of being stopped by a policeman. Recognize that it is *you* who are decreasing the risk, not the racist. Remember *Rule No. 11: Once you have identified someone as racist, no matter what you do, they will always be racist. You will never be able to change their racist behavior.* Once you have identified the shark, whenever they approach your desk, use the nickname (in your head—please not out loud) to remind you on the actions and reactions required to keep this person in check. The use of a nickname will keep you from being your normal, wonderful, adorable self; it will give you the protective gear you need to swim with sharks in dark water.

Shark No. 1 – Horror Boy

Horror Boy is probably the most dangerous shark in the water. In essence, he is the classic sociopath. The best way to understand this person is to read the seminal book *The Sociopath Next Door* by Martha Stout, PhD. In reality, Horror Boy is a menace to everyone, but because of corporate America's acceptance of mistreatment of people of color, they are particularly dangerous to minorities. Horror Boy is a person without conscience, capable of doing anything, with a goal to destroy your ability to make a living, not only in the current environment, but also in any environment. He wants to take you back to where (in his opinion) you should be, unemployed and having less. He tends to follow people he has attacked to continue to enjoy his ability to annihilate. He takes great pleasure in tormenting the weakest, which, in his mind, is usually individuals of color or individuals who he thinks will have little chance of combating his consistent, repeated abuse. The Horror Boy does everything he can do to make your life miserable.

He will cause you to question your ability to do anything right. He gets pleasure out of creating a sense of paranoia.

In my experience, it became so horrible that I would ask fellow coworkers what mood he was in before I went into the office. I started to double-check my work and question the quality of my contributions.

Characteristics:

- Middle management: Horror Boys very seldom make it to senior management in large publicly traded companies because of their behavior. In small companies, they are very successful, usually because they are very astute of collecting dirt on the individuals around them and creating scenarios where they have the upper hand.
- Under fifty: Horror Boys are easily recognizable in their thirties or forties. If you identify Horror Boys in their fifties, it is rare because they tend to be better at hiding their agendas. Also, they are less terrifying in their fifties because they are more likely to take on false ability to feign normal responses and tend to focus on bigger prey than you.
- Mostly men: I have only met one Horror Boy who was a woman, and the organization identified her early, and she was removed. Behavior that is acceptable in a man is not tolerated in a woman. It is very difficult for a woman to be a successful Horror Boy in corporate America. However, if they own the company, heaven help you.
- Affiliation with leadership: Leadership tends not to like these individuals, which is why they do not last in large companies. In reality, Horror Boys are not very adept at their jobs; they are more skilled at controlling information flow, subterfuge, political maneuvering, and just flat-out lying. They usually have several complaints lodged against

them, but they also tend to have very strong relationships with people of power, which they cultivate.

What they will do to you:

- They are very adept at making you look bad and will set you up at a moment's notice. They do this by assigning you to a project and only providing a portion of the requirements, e-mailing senior leadership on your work and not copying you, changing requirements and not telling you, etc. In other words, you never feel you know everything or have everything to be successful or even remotely adequate to complete the task.

- They will give you deadlines that appear impossible to meet. They wait to the last minute to tell the due date for a key assignment. You will have the feeling that they were aware of the requirement earlier, but you cannot prove it is a setup. They will ask you to give the deliverable to them for delivery and then never deliver. They will tell management they never received it or that when received it, it lacked quality and could not be delivered. They will not tell you this until the last possible date and only when they can use the information to destroy your day.

- They will establish an environment where you feel unsafe. Example, as you are walking the halls, they will whisper in someone's ear and look at you. You always feel off-balance.

- They communicate that you are about to be dismissed, should be dismissed, or someone thinks your work is poor. It is always someone else or something they heard. The criticism is vague, almost shadow-like, just enough to haunt you.

- Majority of damage they do is done in private. They will request meetings in which they will denigrate, criticize, or comment on your lack of skill set. They like emotion (from you), so you crying is considered a win for them. If you get mad and fight back, they will inform management, and your behavior will be considered unacceptable to the office. You will be dismissed, and when you request references, they will state that you demonstrated aggressive tendencies in the office.

- They will set up meetings and not show up. Schedule your morning for a particular task, then not give you the work. Since the meeting request was not documented (via a scheduled meeting on your calendar), they leave little recourse for correction. They want you to be seen by others as not having anything to do, so they will do their best to schedule your time for nothing.

- They will tell you that you are not permitted to meet with certain people without their presence and all work must go through them. I even had one Horror Boy tell me that I was not allowed to make calls during the day or use the phone. Their goal is to ensure that you appear sloppy and unqualified. Remember, since they control the flow of information, the less you communicate to other client and staff, the more they control.

- Horror Boys refrain from placing any information or communication in writing. You will find that they rarely e-mail individuals, and most of their e-mails are broadcast emails. In fact, they create few deliverables. They are all talk and no action. It is rare that they will author or coauthor a white paper or any intellectual property. They do not contribute to deliverables; they give orders, not insight.

- Very few Horror Boys are qualified for the job they have. The more qualified and skilled you are, the worse their behavior toward you. However, they will come to you for help on a moment's notice. If they butter you up because they need something, the request will be vague, almost conversational, and (here is the real clue) they will be nice.

How to recognize:

- There is high turnover of the individuals who work for them, no matter the gender or color.
- You will find yourself wanting to check with them, to appease them, to validate that you are okay.
- They tend to enjoy the face-to-face destruction and, as stated earlier, will not place anything in writing.
- They choose the weakest to abuse the most. They are mean, cruel in private, and have been known to say things that are difficult to repeat in public.
- They will lie at a drop of a hat, will make things up.
- They will encourage you to share personal details and use your personal details as weapons against you.
- People will talk about them in private but cozy up to them in public. They are feared by most who work for them.
- In small companies, they become indispensable, usually because they are the only ones who understand or know a client or some key process. They do not share, even with leadership, the key elements of their duties.
- They develop very close relationships with clients and senior management. Horror Boys will do all the work for their leadership and control the flow of information. Senior leadership's view of Horror Boys will be of dependence and their ability to manage the client (totally).
- Horror Boys tend to have tantrums. They do not simply get mad; they behave like children when they are angry. Their tantrums will require some correction by senior management. Usually, their tantrums tend to be based on an expectation that was not met (e.g., bonus was too low, size of office too small, etc.). Their tantrums will have little to do with work, quality, etc. It is always, always about them. Everything is about them.

Survival Guide for Horror Boy:

YOU MUST LEAVE. RUN, DO NOT WALK TO THE NEAREST EXIT. If you find yourself working for and/or near a Horror Boy, start looking for another job immediately. Once you identify that you are working with a Horror Boy, you must do anything and everything you can to move to another division within the company or find a job outside of the company. Until you do leave, do the following:

- Never ever meet with a Horror Boy in private. If a meeting is requested or scheduled, if necessary, call in sick, do whatever you can to cancel. If you do meet, be prepared to be abused. In other words, know that they will say something to put you off, push your buttons, cause issues. Meditate before the meeting. Do whatever you can to ensure that you will stay calm and mentally dismiss everything that is said. Assume that he is lying. Do not trust anything that he says during the meeting. Do not react if he says anything positive or negative—yes, even if he says something positive. If he says something positive, he needs something or he is baiting you.

- Be very aware when a Horror Boy is being nice or ingratiating. It means they need help. You will probably be so happy that they are being nice that you will jump up and help them. *DO NOT DO THIS*. Never share helpful information with a Horror Boy, never give them your inside opinion, never teach them how to do something, never help them complete a task, and never assist them under a deadline. If at all possible, recommend someone else for the task. Talk up the person you recommend so that they will immediately brush you off and run to the new resource.

- Never ever discuss your personal life, issues, opinions on anything with Horror Boy in public or in private. This survival tip also applies to discussing your personal life with anyone in the office. Horror Boy will engage spies to find out anything about you that he can. He will then share this information with a negative slant. I once told Horror Boy that I had ringing in my ears. He told the client I was going deaf. At the next meeting, the client spoke loudly and kept looking at me in the face. I suppose she thought that I could read lips. I had to correct the issue.

- Never tell him you do not feel well, are sick, going to the doctor, etc. If you need to request leave, just state that you have some personal errands to run and, being the individual of "integrity," wish to request leave. Horror Boy will ask again but will simply repeat that you are running errands.

- When he gives you an assignment, immediately send him an e-mail detailing the requirements and copy someone, anyone. He will hate you for this, and he will come to your desk and ask you not to send him information he already knows. Do it anyway, and simply tell him you forgot. If you fear sending him the e-mail, send the e-mail to a peer documenting the assignment and what you have been told to do. Also, make sure you communicate due dates and information provided by Horror Boy. The more detailed, the better. You will be working toward the goals communicated by Horror Boy, and you need to document these goals for protection. Once the assignment is complete or near complete, Horror Boy will tell you that you messed up and missed a major element (one that you were not communicated). You can then forward him the e-mail requesting clarification on the requirements and offering to correct the assignment with the "new" requirements. He will treat you like dirt for doing this, but remember, he is going to treat you like dirt if you had not done this. At least this way, he cannot talk about you to upper management.

- If you are working on an assignment, tell Horror Boy as little as possible; this includes status reports. In the status report, document only the information that is already known. You will be accustomed to creating glowing status reports that document your successes. DO NOT DO THIS. Any successes will encourage Horror Boy to step up his efforts to destroy you.

- Discourage management from complimenting you in front of Horror Boy. If a senior manager makes a comment about an assignment, say thank you and dismiss it as soon as possible. The goal is to stay invisible until you leave. Stay off the radar, stay low, do not make any positive waves. Work in a team and share the credit for your work product with other people. It will be difficult for him to say your work was poor if more than one person can take credit.

- Watch with whom he associates; these will be his potential spies whom he uses to find information on individuals to use against them. They will be easy to spot because someone that you hardly know will suddenly invite you to lunch or stop by your desk and start talking about Horror Boy's or your work, your happiness on the job—you get the picture. Horror Boy's spies will ask you emotion-based questions about your job satisfaction, e.g., are you happy? It does not matter how you answer. If you say yes, they will remind you of the last time you were mistreated. If you say no, they will ask you why, and you will be forced to tell them the last time you were mistreated. Do not answer the question or any question that checks your emotional status.

- Hire a lawyer to assist you with your resignation and negotiate how references will be handled. Heck, hire a lawyer to talk to and discuss possible strategies for survival.

- If necessary, and you have saved money, you may decide to walk away. Every single day you spend with Horror Boy places your future at risk.

<u>Shark No. 2 – Stupid Boy</u>

Stupid Boy is the easiest shark to work with. They are the simplest kind of racist. They just do not want to work with anyone of color at any time. They have a genuine belief that people of color are not genetically bred to do office work. Yes, I just said that. I once asked the assistant dean of a university why there were no blacks in a certain PhD program. His response was that blacks were not genetically bred for higher education. I will not tell you my response. Let's just say that my future at the university was tenuous for a few weeks. The reality that you must understand is Stupid Boy considers this thought a proven fact. When they see a person of color as a peer or on their team, they feel it is their duty to remove them or "cull the herd." They honestly think that your presence is just a mistake, and as soon as they can point it out, it will be corrected.

It is for this reason I use the nickname Stupid Boy because they have a belief system that is stupid. It does not matter how much education or skill they have. A Stupid Boy can be a leader in their field, a senior executive, or one of your peers on the team. Stupid Boys tend to say things and do things that are disruptive. They will do this with the best intentions. Once, the CIO of the company came by to see me to discuss a critical policy. I had stepped away from my desk. The CIO left a note to give her a call. Stupid Boy removed the note and threw it away. The next day he told me that the CIO had left a note and that he had thrown it away. The reasoning, he stated, was that it probably was not important. After all, how could it be important? What in the world would the CIO want with me?

<u>Characteristics:</u>

- <u>Any management level:</u> Stupid Boys can be at any management level. Because their actions are based on a belief system and not on a work ethic, they have no problems rising through the ranks. However, their belief system usually has other issues besides just color; they usually have defined ideas on gender, age, weight, etc. In other words, Stupid Boys tend to have a clear idea in their head as to what makes the world right. Unfortunately, it usually resembles a 1950 concept of life. White men work, woman stay home, women of color are maids, and there are only two genders in the world. Anything outside this image must be removed, either from the office place or their neighborhood, schools, etc. You get the point.

- <u>Over fifty:</u> Stupid Boys tend to be older white men. Stupid Boys are usually from environments where they were taught to be racist. They come from generations of people who had strong beliefs about race and gender. They may or may not be religious. Please do not assume that an extremely religious person is a Stupid Boy. Stupid Boys just believe the old ways were the best ways and the right ways. Young Stupid Boys tend not to make it in the office; their old-fashioned ideas are not tolerated by their peers.

- <u>Mostly men:</u> You will be able to identify them the very first week they join the team and/or when you start your new job. They will show their disapproval about having to work with you. There are a few Stupid Boys who are women; they tend to fall into the same age group. However, Stupid Boys who are women tend not to rise in ranks.

- <u>Affiliation with leadership:</u> Leadership does not care about Stupid Boys. If the leadership are white men, then they will never know they are working with Stupid Boy. He will work with them with the most respect, care, and consideration. He enjoys and takes great pleasure when the world (in his mind) is right. When a Stupid Boy sees a woman (particularly a woman of color) in a leadership position, they literally think that someone must have made a mistake, and they will see it as their job to correct the situation. Or they will see to it that they never ever have to work with a woman in a leadership position. They would rather die. The person who threatened me in the office was a Stupid Boy. They actually see themselves as failures if they are reporting to a person of color or a woman. You could understand their anger, given their belief system, if they are forced to work for a woman of color. It is very rare that you would ever work for a Stupid Boy. They would never hire you, nor ever accept you on their team.

What they will do to you:

- Stupid Boys feel it is their job to make you look bad, but their tools are limited. Mostly it is small stupid actions (e.g., removing notes from your desk, not including you on meetings, etc.).
- They will ignore you. If you provide an insight for a deliverable or job action, it will not be included. If you send an e-mail with edits for a document, they will not be included. You are invisible to them. You have absolutely no value. You have no thoughts or actions worth noticing. They wish you would just go away. In the short term, this behavior is dysfunctional; in the long term these, actions can destroy your future at your job. This is because of the fact that if you are working with a Stupid Boy, your work will never be included, and as such, upper management will start to question your existence (with the encouragement of Stupid Boy).
- If you do receive praise from anyone, they will think it is because you have "natural" talent or was lucky. They do acknowledge that there are some people of color that excel "naturally" at certain skills. They will note that you are unusually articulate or be genuinely surprised that you can write, think, walk, breathe (you get the picture).
- They will take any opportunity they have to diminish you to leadership. Their goal is to restore the order of white men, that perfect order where everyone knew their place.

- They do tend to sabotage, but usually, it is stupid stuff. They have information that you need, and they do not share. A colleague will ask them to include you in a conference call, meeting, etc. They will conveniently forget. Usually, they are eventually corrected.

How to recognize:

- They are old, look old, and have old ways.
- They tend to bring their lunch, eat the same food, and have a pretty definable schedule. In other words, they are simple people.
- Their clothing is middle of the road, and they cannot wait for retirement, and they will probably talk about retirement.
- They will talk to you about how you are not qualified for the job, how you are missing some unique skill, or how you need some additional training. Their acknowledgement of your lack of skill or inability to do something will be stated in a matter-of-fact manner. They will see these statements as simple truths.
- They will not share information. If they speak to you in the office, it is because others are around.
- All the white men will like them and consider them of value in the office. You will see them as an old dinosaur and wonder why other people think they have value.
- They have no particular relationships in the office. They are pretty honest in their work, and they tend to be nine-to-five workers. They leave on time and arrive at the office the same time every day. Their goal is to ensure that the amount of work they have fits into their lifestyle. In other words, these are not flashy people.

Survival Guide for Stupid Boy:

- They must be corrected like a child. They must be corrected early, quickly, and with professional kindness.

They are a nuisance, but they can still do damage. It is better to slap their hand kindly, stating "do not do that again, that is wrong," than to leave them unchecked. Treat them like a bothersome gnat.

- Never send anything in writing to Stupid Boy. He is so stupid he would probably forward it to the president of the company as an example of your incompetence. Any correction must be done verbally and, if possible, with an audience.

- All corrections must be as if you were speaking to a very nice precocious child. The Stupid Boy's belief system is real, and admonishing them for their beliefs is not going to work. You are going to have to approach them on their behavior.

- If necessary, correct "up"; in other words, approach the person above them in a helpful tone. "I need your assistance on a matter: the CIO has asked that I be included in the software acquisition meetings, and Stupid Boy finds it difficult to remember to include me. I know that he is probably busy. Do you have any ideas on how I can encourage him to ensure that I participate?" His leadership will consider this a stupid request because it sounds like a personality issue (you two just do not get along), and he will defer you back to Stupid Boy. But what the leadership will not appreciate (then) is that by calling him or her, you have documented Stupid Boy's behavior. I will make you a bet that within a week, Stupid Boy will tell his leadership that you have not been attending the required meetings. Leadership will say "That's odd because, apparently, you have not included her on the invite list."

- Always be nice to Stupid Boy, no matter what they do. The minute you become angry, they will see this as a genetic flaw, and it will prove that you are unable to be intelligent in the office. They will tell everyone about your inability to be professional. They are always looking for proof to support their belief system. Remember, they are children, simple, and your anger will only provide additional proof to their belief system.

- Remember that Stupid Boy is really stupid. Do not share any work ideas with them or give them support (beyond what is required). They are the poster child for "no good deed goes unpunished."

- If you do, by rare chance, end up working for a Stupid Boy, it will be very important that you immediately set about training them on how they should treat you. One of the rare traits of a Stupid Boy is that they do have exceptions for successful people of color. This is important because, every now and then, they need to explain how certain people of color rise to certain ranks, have money, etc. They do this by removing you from the main color paradigm and giving you an exception. Your training of Stupid Boy will be to demonstrate that you are an exception from their belief system. I know this sounds horrible, you wish you could correct Stupid Boy's belief system. Please refer to Rule No. 11: Once you have identified someone as racist, no matter what you do, they will always be racist. You will never be able to change their racist behavior. To accomplish this goal, discuss your personal life with Stupid Boy, but only to destroy their belief system. Tell them how you spent a year abroad, completed your master's in record time, served on this committee, saved a person's life, belong to an elite club, own a home, boat, first edition, art, etc. It will drive them crazy trying to reconcile what you told them and what they believe. In other words, it is okay to mess with Stupid Boy. You have to convince them that you are the outlier, and as such, they need to place you in the "special" category.

- Make sure, if possible, that management compliments you in front of Stupid Boy. If you win an award, discuss it in front of Stupid Boy's office. The nice thing about Stupid Boy is that he is never jealous of you. You are not considered a white man, so by his belief system, you are not even a part of his world. You do not deserve his comparison or jealously. You are doing this to move yourself outside his belief system. You must become the outlier, the exception to his rule.

- Stupid Boys are pretty easy to manage, but they must be managed every single day. When Stupid Boy makes a comment that is derogatory, you must correct it within sixty seconds. If he makes that comment in front of anyone, you must correct immediately. Although a child, they can still do damage to your career. Stupid Boy's belief system is constant, solid, and real to him. It is important that you remember that the correction you did yesterday may need to be repeated tomorrow. He has the nickname Stupid Boy for a reason.

Shark No. 3 – The Family Man

The family man is one of the unique sharks. They are the person that takes on the responsibility to do what the racist cannot. The Family Man takes on the responsibility to act out the feeling of the racist. Permit me to give you an example. Let's say you live next door to a family, and the father of this family is a racist. He uses the "n" word, talks about immigrants, and continually complains how people of color have destroyed this country. However, he never does anything physical and never threatens you or harms you. He is just your next-door neighbor who is racist. This racist has a young son. This young son has torn up your garden, hit your daughter, and shouted unacceptable language at your spouse. You have complained to the son's father, trying to correct, but nothing worked. The young son is doing what his father is too much of a coward to do. He is being encouraged by his father, taught by his father, and applauded by his father. The Family Man is the son. He works for a racist or with a racist, and although the racist just talks about you (in private), the Family Man acts out the anger, frustration, and evil of the racist. He thinks he is doing a good thing. He is doing what he should do to protect the "natural order." He is fulfilling his duties as the dedicated prodigal son.

Now you are going to ask me the difference between the racist and the Family Man. The Family Man is manipulated, encouraged, and directed by the racist (the dominant shark). In reality, for the Family Man, you are actually working with two racists, but only the Family Man is visible. This is a difficult racist to manage and correct, but each and every time he does something, he shares it with the racist (the dominant shark) and the racist spurs him on. For the Family Man, you will need to also identify the dominant shark. The dominant shark is less important, but understanding who he is will help anticipate the activities of the Family Man.

You may wonder why we focus on the Family Man and not the dominant shark. The dominant shark is a coward and is basically pointless. You would not focus on the dominant shark no more than you would focus on the boy's father. If you have approached the father, you found him without remorse and basically unhelpful in curbing the behavior of his son. You also thought that there was a glint in his eye, and he was aware of his son's behavior, approved of it, and was quite proud. The dominant shark is no different. Without the Family Man, the dominant shark would simply be an angry unhappy racist. Dominant sharks say things (in private) and have a real hate for individuals of color, but they do not have the courage to act it out. Because of this, you should focus on the Family Man. It is the Family Man's action that you will need to react to and correct.

Characteristics:

- Lower management: Family Men tend to be in lower management and may work for the dominant shark. However, the dominant shark is always in a leadership position above the Family Man and understands that certain (racist) behavior may place their career at risk and will recruit a Family Man to do their business. Family Men seldom make it to upper management. They also may have followed the dominant shark to several different jobs. They are prevalent regardless the size of the company. Dominant sharks can exist anywhere at any time. The good news is that dominant sharks normally recruits only one Family Man at a time.

- <u>Under fifty:</u> Family Men are under fifty. Meeting a Family Man over fifty is extremely rare because they tend to support only one or two dominant sharks in their career. Because they support dominant sharks, they stagnate at the middle management level. The dominant shark needs to be in the superior position and will give the Family Man a raise but rarely a promotion (unless the dominant shark receives a higher promotion). Eventually, the dominant shark will drop them because they no longer serve the purpose or are too old. Dominant sharks like young Family Men; they are easier to manipulate and happy (this is important) to do their bidding. Family Men will then live out their career in the exact place where they were dropped by the dominant shark.

- <u>Can be any gender:</u> I have met Family Men of all genders. These are individuals used because of their ability to be manipulated by the dominant shark. Female dominant sharks tend to have other females as their chosen Family Men. However, the female Family Man is easier to identify; they are very loyal to the dominant shark and will communicate their loyalty to everyone and will admit that most of their actions are at the bidding of the dominant shark. Male Family Men, tend not to admit that they are being controlled by an older dominant shark.

- <u>Affiliation with leadership:</u> Family Men only associate with their dominant shark. The will spend time together, visit the client together, go to meetings together. Because the Family Man spends so much time with their dominant shark, other leadership will not know them very well.

Other leadership in the office will simply see the Family Man as the dominant shark's go-to-guy.

What they will do to you:

- Family Men act out the feelings of the dominant shark. They will say things and do things that are as mean and as destructive as the dominant shark will permit and encourage. Their activities will be right on the edge of aggression. The gauge on what they can do depends entirely on the secret "at-a-boys" they receive from their dominant shark.

- They are destructive in a mischievous malicious manner, like the next-door neighbor's son who destroys your garden or keys your car. You will find their destruction unsettling and almost to the edge of threatening but never to the point of feeling your career is at risk. And herein lies the issue because if you did not recognize them as the Family Man, you may consider them more threatening than they are.

- They do property damage. In other words, the Family Man wants to ruin your reputation, not your career. They do not know how to ruin a career, but they can make you appear difficult to work with. They want you in a stage of anger and frustration. Nothing would make them happier than having you frustrated.

- Family Men are focused and obvious. Once they are given a mission by the dominant shark, they will "hop to it" immediately. Unlike other sharks, they will announce their activity. They will stop you in the hall, ask you to step into their office (if they have one) or the conference room. They will then start to key your car (say or do something that causes you frustration).

- Family Men will only approach you when they are on a mission. Otherwise, why bother? They do not normally interface or work with you. Like the little boy who tore up the garden, they want you to know it was them who did the damage, and the damage should be obvious. They want the dominant shark to see you mad, frustrated, and angry.

- Family Men are pranksters. They will do things to bother you: ask you an inane question as you are getting on the elevator, approach your desk with a made-up problem, or send you an e-mail that has no real meaning. Example: The e-mail may be the minutes of a meeting that you were not invited to attend, but your name is mentioned, and you are copied. They want you to come to their desk and say, "What is this about?" Then they will toy with you for a few minutes, not really answering the question, creating more vague statements. The goal is (once again) to frustrate you.
- Family Men like to do their acts in public and private. They do not care, whatever it takes to get to you.

How to recognize:

- Family Men appear to do very little except follow the dominant shark.
- When they are not following the dominant shark, they are doing something the dominant shark asked them to do.
- They appear incompetent or less than competent. You may question their existence, what they do and why they do it.
- You may not recognize them at first, but as time goes by, it will feel like they poke you on a regular basis.
- You start to try to avoid them, you find them a nuisance, and the statements they make appear as if they were goading you (they are).
- They hang out with the dominant shark and appear almost in glee when the dominant shark shows up.
- They want to appear professional, very professional. After all, the dominant shark has placed so much trust in them. They will admire this trust and state as much (sometimes often).

- Their loyalty to the dominant shark will be more important than their job. They will appear busy and very focused when given a task by the dominant shark.
- They will not have relationships with other leadership, except at the behest of the dominant shark.

Survival Guide for the Family Man:

- For the Family Man, you must pretend that you are the United States, and they are a small country with the potential for nuclear weapons. Your reactions to their actions must be appropriate for the issue. If they say something incorrect, simply correct. If they do something that causes damage, request that they fix or repair.
- If they do not respond to the request to correct (a statement) or repair (the damage), treat them no differently than the son of the racist. Go to their father and state the issue (factually) and ask for help for the correction. The dominant shark will gloat and scoff. But place the request anyway. Under no circumstance are you to take any of the actions of the Family Man to human resources (HR). If you do this, you have escalated an innocent game designed by the dominant shark. Do not underestimate the dominant shark's willingness to protect the Family Man. In the act of protecting the Family Man, their bond will be even closer, and the future shenanigans will be even worse.
- In most cases, unless you work directly with the Family Man, try to avoid as much as possible. If you cannot avoid, never meet with them alone.
- E-mails, documentation, and deliverables are no issue with the Family Man. They tend to go for the emotional response. This is why they do not focus on career damage. They focus on achieving an emotional response. The more frustration you show, the happier they (both the dominant shark and the Family Man) are. This is why you *must* keep your emotions under check and respond in accordance to the act itself.

Shark No. 4 – The Political Hire

Once I was working on a large outsourcing team in Europe, and one of my team members was a Political Hire. He was the most incompetent person I had ever worked with. He had absolutely no experience for his assignment, and every time we (the team) needed something, he had disappeared. When he would return, he would say he was meeting with so-and-so (major name-drop). Over time, I started to really dislike him, and unfortunately, there were times where the dislike was noticeable. As a woman of color, I had been taught that you had to pull your weight, be at least minimally qualified. No one had ever been given a job based on a contact, especially a job they could not do. In white corporate America, the Political Hire is a common occurrence. Sometimes people are hired because of who they know, who they are related to, a friend or relative of a client. Whatever the reason, they are hired and put to work.

The problem is that, as women of color, we are not accustomed to working with people who, on the surface, do not appear to warrant their position. We worked hard for our opportunity, and darn it, everyone else should work as hard or harder. In white corporate America, this is not true. There are many reasons a person is given a job, and qualifications is only one of many reasons. My hope is that you experience a Political Hire early in your career so that you can understand that there are all kinds of sharks in the water.

Anyway, back to Europe. On the second day of our arrival, the regional vice president called a team meeting to hand out assignments. There were key assignments, and a few of us were vying for leadership positions. While the presentation was given on the components of the assignments, I started to watch Political Hire. I noticed that he was totally lost, and he was following the tone of the presenter. If the presenter said something in a positive tone, he would repeat the statement and agree. In a negative tone, he would emphasize the negative side of the statement. For the first time in my working career, I started to understand one thing: There are many animals in the jungle, and some of them do not work for a living, but that does not mean that they do not have a difficult life.

While I was recovering from jet lag, the Political Hire was on the phone making political connections. While I was relaxed at the meeting hoping for a great assignment, the Political Hire working so hard to "please" and follow the speaker. I watched him during the meeting, and he was working so hard. I started to understand that how a person acquires a job is not my business. But I had treated him poorly because of my expectations, and my relationship with him had to be fixed. I started to treat him with the respect of his position, and as a result, I learned a great deal. It is important, as you move up the ladder, that you understand that it is not your job to ensure that your paradigm of equality is forced on the world. Over time, I have learned that fighting for humanity is more important than fighting for equality (but that's another book).

Working with a Political Hire is absolutely no threat to your career unless you have the prejudices that we (as people of color) were given as children. We were told and taught that success had to be earned, worked for, achieved through education and hard work. In reality, in corporate white America, success comes in so many different ways. But once a person is successful, their position should be appreciated and respected. Political Hires are so busy being political they are no threat to a person of color. However, how we treat them can create a career threat for us.

Characteristics:

- <u>Any management:</u> Political Hires can occur at any level, even as a president or CEO. Individuals who are placed in positions for reasons other than skill set are Political Hires.
- <u>Under fifty:</u> Most Political Hires are under fifty, but they can be of any age. Older Political Hires are rare. If you

find yourself working with an older Political Hire, they are usually provided with a senior leadership position.

- <u>Can be any gender:</u> Most Political Hires are men. I have never met a woman Political Hire, but it would be nice to meet one. It would mean that the business environment is getting closer to gender equality. I can remember watching television as a child, and my mother said, "Do you know when black entertainers will be equal? It will be when you see bad ones on television." We were watching a black stand-up comic that was phenomenal, and my mother was saying that it is when we have bad stand-up comics of color that the entertainment industry would have achieved equality. So I would love to see a female Political Hire, especially a female of color Political Hire.
- <u>Affiliation with leadership:</u> Political Hires work very hard to ensure that they are connecting with leadership. They are supportive, agreeable, and using their time for political connections with higher leadership. That is their skill set. They ignore their peers and lower leadership. They understand that their position is based on connections, and they work full time to ensure that their connections for survival are solid.

What they will do to you:

- Political Hires will only attack you if you did what I did, which was to question their reason for living. If you appreciate their status and understand that their position is as viable as yours, they will leave you alone.

How to recognize:

- They are constantly dropping names and connecting with higher ups. If you demonstrate that you know someone they need, they will connect with you.
- They will not do much or any work. Normally, they do not have the skill set for the job they were given. They will not

ask you to do their work because they will not be given any work. If you have a Political Hire on your team or working for you, understand this, and leave them alone.

- They will not be where you expect them to be. They have a different agenda; they will be networking, attending a higher-up meeting, having lunch, etc. Everything they do will be to support their "required" political agenda.

<u>Survival Guide for the Political Hire:</u>

- *<u>LEAVE THEM ALONE.</u>* Every single jungle has a hyena or a jackal. You and I have been told that real workers are hunters. We are strong, dedicated, educated, skilled individuals who have worked awfully hard for our positions. It is hard for us to watch a scavenger. But white corporate America understands that there are all kinds of sharks in the water, and each have their own value. A Political Hire may not be a shark that we appreciate, but they are still a shark. Butting it in the nose is not a good idea. Its swimming style may not be glamorous, but it is still a shark.
- Do not give them any work unless they request the work or a higher-up requests that you delegate to them. Even then, please check to ensure that they are comfortable. However, even though you need to be careful, you do not need to be obsequious. Do not do any work for them. Do not help them look good. Do not become their friend. Do not associate with them after work, before work, during work. They will approach you if they need something.
- Political Hires can be racist, but they do not care. Their pecking order is based on politics, which is a colorless, genderless world. If a black woman was vice president of sales, and they needed their support, the Political Hire would be right there with compliments or whatever was needed to garner the VP's support.

<u>Shark No. 5 – The Gatekeeper</u>

This species of shark is rare and almost extinct. The last few remaining Gatekeepers work in old institutions, surrounded by things that remind them of why they are or were great. Gatekeepers are the sharks responsible for ensuring that minorities not gain entry into clubs, certain degree programs, position or titles in areas where minorities, especially women, have not been able to gain access. These are the firsts remaining in our society. Whenever you hear about the first black or woman doing something, in today's world, it is because they have successfully broken through the ceiling(s) maintained by Gatekeepers. Once a ceiling is removed, the Gatekeeper is nullified.

When I entered graduate school, I chose a major that I thought I would really enjoy. As I started to take class, another discipline caught my passion. The more courses I took in the field, the more I knew that this was where I was supposed to be. Finally, I approached the dean and inquired about transferring. After a few discussions, the transfer was approved, and I moved into the chosen discipline thinking I had done the best thing ever. The next day I was walking down the hall, and the department chair of my chosen program approached me. He said to me that I would never graduate under his watch, that no blacks had ever graduated with a degree in this area, and no black ever would. He strongly suggested that I return to my first choice, but he continued that he had spoken with that department chair, and he did not want me either. He also suggested that given the fact that so many people were upset by my transfer, perhaps I should look for another school within the university to apply. I responded that I wanted a business degree. He said that may not be possible. As he walked away, he said that he hoped I kept my grades up.

I had met Gatekeepers before, but this Gatekeeper was extremely vigilant in ensuring that the standards set by the university in terms of color and gender were kept. I survived and graduated but not without help. I had finished my classwork but found that working on my dissertation was difficult because of the Gatekeeper. I finally gave up and decided to quit and, for the first time since I started, did not register for any classes. As I sat home and cried, realizing the gravity of my decision, an angel called. It was the new department chair. The Gatekeeper had retired, and the new chair was a woman. She noted that I had not registered (yet) and suggested that I hurry and get that done because, she continued, she was determined that I graduate as soon as possible. Eight months later, I was standing in front of my dissertation committee receiving applause. Tears rolled down my face. Sometimes, no matter how hard you try, there are things that you cannot accomplish alone.

Gatekeepers are cruel. If it is a goal that is part of your dream, drives your life, ignites your passion, a Gatekeeper can crush you. Of all the acts of racism, the cruelest is the denial of a dream. These individuals are chartered with keeping the status quo, maintaining the balance, and destroying dreams. Historically, it has been the Gatekeepers that have done the most damage to our country and even the world. Think about what we lost when a brilliant individual of color was denied admittance to a university or a position in a company in which they could have made a difference if they had been fully embraced. What type of world would not want to use intellectual capital because of color or gender or any other physical attribute that has absolutely nothing to do with the value of a mind.

Historically, Gatekeepers create the most damage, not because of what they deny an individual, but what they keep from the world. We matter. Everybody matters. It is the Gatekeepers that we remember most. Gatekeepers have become nearly extinct because so many ceilings have been removed because of the sacrifice individuals have made to prove them wrong. Being the first to pass a Gatekeeper is a job unto itself. It is hard enough to pursue a PhD, but try it with an entire department working to have you fail. Imagine being the first black vice president and having many of your peers working to have you fail. This is why when you hear the phrase "first black" or "first woman," you should take note and imagine the number of Gatekeepers they had to cross to achieve their goal. And then you should give thanks because the first always removes the Gatekeeper, making it easier for all that follows.

Characteristics:

- <u>Leadership positions:</u> Gatekeepers have leadership positions or are in positions of authority. They are usually high enough on the leadership level to set policy.
- <u>Over fifty:</u> Most Gatekeepers are near retirement or past retirement. You will never work for a Gatekeeper. Their goal is to ensure that you never work with them or near them.
- <u>Can be any gender:</u> Gatekeepers can be any gender, but most are men. Gatekeepers who are women normally take on the role of passive racist because they rarely have a senior leadership position necessary with enough power to maintain a gate.
- <u>Affiliation with leadership:</u> Gatekeepers are normally so powerful that most individuals seek affiliation with them. Just as they can close doors, they can open them as well. When I took my comprehensive exam for my degree, the academic team that graded my exam stated that they wish they had invested more time in my academic career. It was not until they finally tested me that they realize that I had value. But because all those affiliated with the Gatekeeper had followed his directions, trying to ensure that I did not graduate with a degree in their discipline, they had not recognized the value I brought to the department.

What they will do to you:

- Gatekeepers will deny you your dream. These are not the normal racist barriers in which you can leave the organization and find a job at another organization. These are the racists who literally keep you from the next level or next personal benchmark. These are the people who keep you from flying. They will knock the wind out of your sails.

How to recognize:

- Gatekeepers are the easiest of all the racists to recognize. They will tell you who they are and what they are about to do.
- They are the old sharks in the water and have usually been with the institution or company for years. They tend to be admired and feared by their peers and carry a lot of weight in how the organization is managed.

Survival Guide for the Gatekeeper:

- *FIGHT FOR YOUR DREAM.* Dreams are worth fighting for. Once a Gatekeeper says no, immediately find an alliance. Do not walk away or give up. Unfortunately, Gatekeepers do not care if they are called out. They are quite proud of their stance. In this regard, you are very fortunate because the world has changed (since 1950) and Gatekeepers are no longer honored for what they do. As a dying breed of shark, nearly extinct, their ability to maintain the gates are less than it was years ago. Today your ability to communicate their archaic thinking gives you an edge. Tell everyone and anyone what this person has said and what they are denying you.
- Once you have outed a Gatekeeper, it is very important that you maintain a perfect image. In other words, you must be overqualified for whatever you are fighting for. I know this seems unfair, but you will be scrutinized, and any flaw will be used against you. The reality of being the first, and it only takes one, to remove a Gatekeeper is that you need to be a special warrior, one that can weather

the slings and arrows that will be thrown. The level of perfection required is near impossible. But remember, only those that are near perfect rise to face Gatekeepers. The fact that you are there means you have already made and surpassed the grade.

- Removal of a Gatekeeper takes time. So your dream will be delayed once you decide to fight. My Gatekeeper added four years to my dissertation. So please be prepared to have your dream delayed while you fight the Gatekeeper. Believe me when I say when you achieve your dream, the time delay will be meaningless.
- It will cost you something. Remember that as the first, the removal of the Gatekeeper will come at a cost. You will be tired, older, maybe poorer, and alone (at times). But when you finally removed the Gatekeeper, please understand that all those who follow may not know what you have done but will be indebted to you. You have done something quite special, and we all thank you.

Shark No. 6 – The Passive Racist (a.k.a. The Buffer)

Passive Racists are the puppies of the jungle. They are kind, thoughtful, considerate individuals who do not know that they are racists. They have a discomfort with certain situations, a preference for certain people, and a decision process that has embedded values that they are unable to articulate. They are the perfect poster children for Rule No. 8. Their visceral response to minorities drives how they think and the decisions they make. They have a level of discomfort that they are unable to clarify or communicate. This discomfort drives their behavior around minorities.

The Passive Racist is an individual who does not have the power but has enough humanity not to overtly act out their feelings. They just do not want to help you. They have too much of a conscience to state these feelings, but their feelings of discomfort are so strong that these feelings determine how they interact with you.

I had an assignment to develop a business case for a new service/ product designed to support an industry that had been hit hard by legislation. The service/product would not only support compliance activities but would also reduce the customer's risk within the industry. I enjoyed writing the business case and decided to recommend a value-pricing strategy. I had developed the various algorithms required, and the next step was to identify the revenue expected for the financial models. I was given a team, and on this team was a very kind and professional white woman. I walked her through the algorithms and, in detail, using examples, showed her how to calculate expected revenue. She listened, was attentive, demonstrated that she understood. I returned to my desk to work on the other components of the business case, awaiting her numbers for the final analysis. A few days later, I stopped by to check on her. She had done nothing. Not a single calculation was complete.

I know that many of you reading this probably assume that she just did not know how to do the calculations. But if you are a minority, as noted when I discussed Rule No. 8, you have seen this behavior, and although perplexing, you understand passive-aggressive racist behavior. After all, she has performed tasks that were more difficult than this task. Another great example is having a cashier that, for some reason, is unable to achieve an approval for your credit card. They hand it back to you with this very sad look, stating it had been rejected. You call for the manager, and they run your card with no problem. The cashier looks at the manager and, with a confused smile, starts packing your groceries. You recognize the behavior. It happens to you all the time.

So I was standing there looking at her sad, confused face. I asked her why. I asked her why she did not request assistance. She just stared at me. She could not explain why. She just said she could not do the numbers. I asked her if she understood that I had set up the formula and it was a simple spreadsheet. She said she knew but she could not do it. I ended up doing the calculations myself.

Now this passive-aggressive behavior is very dangerous. She did not approach me and tell me that she was having problems. Her goal, whether she wishes to admit it or not, was to undermine the project. This little puppy may be cute, but they like peeing on your carpet, tearing up your favorite shoes, and doing other puppy damage. Under that sweet kind face lies a mischievous creature that can still do damage to your career. The Passive Racist waited as long as possible before telling me that she had done nothing. As a matter of fact, I had been checking with her regularly, and she had smiled and told me everything was fine. Only when I went looking for her deliverable to complete the assignment did she finally admit she had done nothing. What she did not know was that I did not wait until the last moment to check with her. I had assigned a due date that gave me some flexibility, given the final numbers, to tweak the revenue projections for the business case. I was able to finish the business case on time and with the content that I had hoped for. I am sure that she was not very happy when I submitted the business case. I am also sure that she did not know why she was not happy.

Characteristics:

- <u>Middle management / Worker bees:</u> The Passive Racist is normally a middle manager, a team member, a cashier, bank teller, etc. They are usually individuals who had very little power in the organization. They are the worker bees. The only power they are able to exercise is the power to deny. They can deny assistance, deny approval through some passive nonaction, or deny success by not performing a task which may be critical to a deliverable.
- <u>Any age:</u> Passive Racist can be any age. They can be a twenty-two-year-old cashier or a sixty-four-year-old

social worker. The older they are, the more mature their passive behavior tactics are. A sixty-four-year-old guidance counselor will have you convinced that the reason your daughter did not register in time for an academic test or scholarship was the completed application getting lost in the mail, missing the required school code, was entirely you or your daughter's fault. They do this with the most helpful smile and tone. For a second, just one second, you actually believe them. But then you see behind the smile and note all the mistakes and issues that seem to be just beyond their control, and you see them for who they really are. They are that puppy that has just peed on your Oriental carpet.

- <u>Tend to be women:</u> Majority of Passive Racists are women. Male racists are more comfortable with their feelings of hate and would rather be overt than pretend for a second to mess up. If they are male, they are older and have a job that provides a lot of freedom for how they treat customers. In other words, they have little oversight. He could be that male car salesman who neglects to tell you about a factory discount or the male real estate agent who fails to show you your dream home because it resides in a certain neighborhood.

- <u>Affiliation with leadership:</u> The Passive Racist does not really care about leadership. They are the worker bees. They are very happy with their 1–3 percent annual raise and are content with where they are. They have little power or authority, which is one of the main reasons why their aggression is passive. They tend to be very nice people, and the leadership in the office will question you if you complain about their work.

What they will do to you:

- They will wait until past the due date to tell you that something that is very important to you has failed. They will do this in a manner that it has some harmful impact. Then they will gleefully watch your reaction.

- If the Passive Racist is in a leadership position, they will place themselves in the middle of your assignments and work effort. The goal will be (through their passive aggression) to mess you up. Now remember, they do not consciously understand why they get so much glee from your failure, but they need to do this.

- They will destroy your career with kindness. The acts of passive-aggressive behavior will appear annoying, at first, until it costs you something of value.

How to recognize:

- If you associate with an individual who consistently causes you a loss of some type through actions that always have an explanation, you have met a Passive Racist.

- The Passive Racist is not above feigning lack of knowledge or loss of memory for the issues that cause you pain. "Oh, I did not know that Friday was the cutoff date for adding your child to your health plan. I am so sorry, but you will have to wait until next year." "Yes, the graduate scholarship was available, but your transcript never came . . . I see, you personally delivered your transcript last Friday. Well, it must have been misplaced." "Yes, that house was on the market when you were looking, but I did not know you wanted to live there." All this will be said with the most calming voice and delivered with a concerned smile.

- Explanations for mistakes will be based on a nebulous element, something that is quite plausible. Only after a number of them occur will you recognize them for who they are, the Passive Racist.

- The Passive Racist is like the beautiful flower in the jungle that also causes paralysis. They appear helpful, agreeable, will even appear to go out of their way. Their goal is to make it look that they are being very helpful. Think of the cashier that has run your credit card four times, and then holds it up in the air and says in a loud enough voice for everyone in line to hear, "Hey, I think this card has been rejected." Then he tries another card, and the same thing happens. But all the while he is appearing to show empathy that you are obviously a minority and, like most minorities, you cannot handle your credit. The cashier is so sorry that you are having such a difficult financial time and may even comfort you for your assumed poverty.

- Unlike the other sharks in the water, there is no real benefit for the Passive Racist in their behavior. They will not receive a raise because of your failure or any other benefit. Their entire payback for their actions is the feeling they derive from it.

- With the exception of the passive-aggressive racist behavior, Passive Racists are pretty nice people. You may have had lunch with them, invited them over your house, go on play dates with your children. It may take you a while to figure out who they are, but if you consistently see a loss of something every time they are around, they are Passive Racists.

Survival Guide for the Passive Racist:

- Do not give anyone more than three times to mess with you, regardless of the reason. Do not wait to confirm that you are dealing with a Passive Racist. On the third strange failure, you are to jump in and fix the issue yourself. After you fix the issue, do not use the Passive Racist for anything.

- Never ever spank or kick the puppy in private or public. In private, you will feel bad; in public, you will look bad. Because Passive Racists are seen as puppies, please do not kick them in the office. Yelling or correcting the puppy that just peed on your Oriental carpet may be understandable, but to the passerby, you look like an ogre.

- Do not argue or correct Passive Racists. Like the cashier in the store, simply call for someone else (manager, another cashier) for assistance. Say "I think my credit card works, but it does not appear to work with this machine. Could you try it on your machine? Thank you." In other words, beat them at their own puppy game. Smile and be very— yes, very—nice.

- If they do interject themselves into your work or life, consider them a risk, and take a risk-adverse approach. Give them fake deadlines for work. Deadlines that will enable you to complete the work when they suddenly confess that they could not complete the assignment or completed the assignment wrong because the directions you gave them were confusing or they decided that your directions were wrong and did the assignment in a manner that you cannot use.

- If the work is important, remove them from the project or give them something to do that is so innocuous that you do not care what they do. Never tell them a piece of material has meaning or is important to the work product. Treat them the same way you treat the cashier who messed up your credit card. Try not to use the cashier again (get in another line) or pay cash.

Shark No. 7 – The Absolute Incompetent

There are many people who are incompetent, and there are times, in all our professional lives, we are performing a task that we do not know how to do. This temporary incompetence is acceptable, and most people work very hard to ensure that this time is minimized. We tend not like being in a position of not knowing how to do the task that we have been assigned and will use whatever resources at our disposal to learn. However, there are some people who are professionally incompetent. These are the Absolute Incompetents. The normal feeling that you and I feel in a state of unknowing is the Absolute Incompetent's normal state. They have no initiative to learn the task; they prefer to either manipulate others to do the work for them or blame the lack of normal day work progress or accomplishments on anyone and anything else. They are the vultures of the corporate environment.

The Absolute Incompetent are of no importance in the office and normally cause minimal harm. Like vultures, they normally do not bother the healthy, but because we are unfamiliar with the state of incompetence (when we are incompetent, we are more likely to get fired), we have a very difficult time correctly responding to the Absolute Incompetent. The Absolute Incompetent preys on individuals of color because of our gullibility and inexperience. They see us as their prime target or remedy for the times when their incompetence is visible to the organization. Another important note is that Absolute Incompetents tend to flock together. When you identify one, all their associations will also be incompetent.

I had the pleasure of working with one Absolute Incompetent. She was so bad that when the team had conference calls with her, we would literally laugh and make jokes when she left the call. She added no value to the work stream but was the director of a component of our deliverable. I made one major mistake: I let her know that I thought she was an Absolute Incompetent. I did not know or even understand that very much like the Political Hire, my job was to treat her as if she were competent. About a year later, I was on another work team and was assigned a task. The Absolute Incompetent insisted that I was assigned a task that I had never performed before, and to make life more difficult, the task required a solution be presented to a Fortune 10 client in two days.

I panicked. As a woman of color, I knew that my incompetence would not be tolerated. If I could not deliver a quality solution and present it in two days, then my career would be over. What the Absolute Incompetent underestimated was the dogged determination of a woman of color. Living under stress is almost a norm for a woman of color in the corporate ranks. I had never had the luxury of residing in a state of unknowing. My entire corporate career had been staying steps ahead of what was needed. My problem was *not* that I did not know what to do but identifying what I needed to do to successfully meet the objectives of the task.

This was a while ago, when there were still bookstores that carried a large selection of technical manuals. I purchased about $400 of manuals and went to my hotel room. Studying the manuals, I was able to develop a solution. I then called a few friends who had a good understanding of the technology and ran my thoughts by them. Using their input, by 4:00 a.m. of the day of the presentation, I was done. I delivered the presentation. It was "freakin'" perfect. With no sleep for forty-eight hours, I had accomplished the impossible. I sat across the client and delivered. The Absolute Incompetent was livid and started to question the viability of what I had proposed. Now remember, she worked for the same company as I, and we were supposed to be on the same team. But the strategy had failed. I had learned a valuable lesson. Never ever tell the Absolute Incompetent that you recognize them as the corporate vulture.

Characteristics:

- <u>Any level of management:</u> The Absolute Incompetent can rise to any level, with the exception of leadership positions that require skill and a continued knowledge investment. It would have to be a very good Absolute Incompetent to be a chief information officer (CIO). It is possible, but it would have to be a highly dysfunctional organization. Because unlike a Political Hire, they are not placed in a position; they claw their way up the ladder. They are easier to identify in middle management. Only a small percentage make it to upper management or leadership positions. In really dysfunctional organizations, or organizations that tend to have the highest amount of racism, they can rise very fast.

- <u>Over forty:</u> Most Absolute Incompetents are in their forties and above. Today's younger generations tend to have resources to support knowledge sharing and take more pleasure in learning on the job. The Absolute Incompetent does not believe in hard work and believes in a show-up-and-fake-it philosophy. Yes, they do show up, but they do not believe in work. If they are young, they are more likely to use their physical skills to succeed (I will let your imagination run with that one).

- <u>Can be any gender:</u> Absolute Incompetents can be any gender and are equally dangerous, regardless of gender. Because they do not believe in work, their appearance will be pretty average. Do not expect an Absolute Incompetent to stand out, except for the fact that there will be times when they will obviously appear very dumb (lots of times).

- <u>Affiliation with leadership:</u> The Absolute Incompetent will take credit for anything that moves and steal credit from anyone they can. They seek leadership positions, for they understand (or at least think) that the higher they go, the easier it is to steal every single idea and work effort from their peers and the poor individuals assigned to them. They are vultures. Because of this, they will be included on leadership activities only when required. Everyone will know what and who they are, but because of their ability to set people up and steal work, the organization will find it difficult to remove them, and they will exist until the organization either fails or they accidently cross the line. My Absolute Incompetent was fired a year later. I asked around why, and no one would tell me. No one would say a word. I assumed she had crossed the line. She probably preyed on the wrong person.

What they will do to you:

- The Absolute Incompetent has two basic strategies:

  1. They steal every single idea or work effort from anyone who is unfamiliar with their practices or too dumb to know who they are; and
  2. They believe that as long as someone else is doing more poorly than they, their incompetence will escape notice. To do this, they will set you up royally to get you fired. Yes, their strategy is to get you fired. They know that it takes a lot of energy for an organization to fire someone, and while the firing is taking place, they do not have to do any work.

How to recognize:

- They are very easy to spot. They look dumb, they act dumb, and they are more likely dumb. You will be amazed at how comfortable they are in being dumb. They will never apologize for not knowing something. They think that everyone works for them.
- Like vultures, they prefer the weak and sickly. In other words, they are particularly attracted to taking advantage of minorities (focusing on women). If they are in a leadership position, they are more likely to hire a minority for their team or suggest that a minority is moved to their team. They appear nice and supportive as a leader until you realize that you had to help them turn on their computer, open a spreadsheet, or check their e-mail. Their level of incompetence will astonish you, but because they are your "boss," you will feel obligated to assist.
- If the Absolute Incompetent is not in a leadership position, they will reach out to the minority on their work team. They will talk work and ask questions. They will focus on your ideas and thoughts, and then immediately run to management and share everything you said as if it were

their idea. They will also catalogue your mistakes; just in case they do something really stupid, they can highlight your errors to management to take the focus off them.

- Their success is through subterfuge. They will use people, lie, blame others, and if you are unfortunate to work for them, they will blame you for any issue with their work. If blaming you does not work, they will try their best to ensure that you fail quickly. Then they will hire someone else who is more amenable to ensuring their strategy of success through incompetence.

- They will only associate with other Absolute Incompetents. You will not see them with the up-and-coming "thought leaders." They will *never* associate with the "smart people." They may talk to them to steal ideas, but generally, they are more comfortable hanging out with other vultures. They tend to run in gangs or flocks or herds. They associate with one another not for comfort, but for ideas for stealing and setting people up. Besides, it helps to have an alibi, and they need similar-minded individuals to share ideas for committing their crimes.

- They will delegate as much as possible. Or they will work with support. They very seldom do anything without someone's support for the two reasons noted above. They will either steal the individual's work effort, or if the assignment goes poorly, they will ensure that their supporter takes full blame. The blame will be so horrendous that it will be considered a reason to place the individual on probation or to start some type of disciplinary action.

Survival Guide for the Absolute Incompetent:

- *FIND A NEW JOB.* First, if you see a lot of Absolute Incompetents in the organization, that is an indication that the organization is sick and failing. Run, do not walk to the nearest opportunity.

- Do not ever give them any indication that you think they are dumb. Assure them that it is very common not to know how to turn on their computer and that you do not mind doing it for them if it makes their life easier.

- Until you leave, assume that your job will be to not only do their job, but also to ensure that management thinks they are doing all the work. If they see you as an asset, they will not immediately eliminate you but may keep you around long enough for you to find another position.

- Do not tell anyone that you are looking. Do not tell even your friends in the office. The Absolute Incompetent is always checking to ensure that you understand your place. It is impossible for you to be perfect, so it is only a matter of time before you say something inappropriate. "I thought everyone knew how to text" or "Just push the on button, it is right there in front of your face." When this happens, hide for about thirty minutes, and maybe they will forget. After all, they are dumb.

- Working with an Absolute Incompetent is easier to manage if they are a peer. In this case, do not share any ideas, do not chit chat, do not have lunch, and do not walk by their desk. In other words, physical proximity is dangerous. You see, Absolute Incompetents are extremely skilled at getting you share ideas or getting you volunteer to help them. So it is better to avoid them like the plague.

- Absolute Incompetents are opportunity racists. Again, like vultures, they prey on the weak and sickly. Minorities are considered weak, more vulnerable segment of the corporate white culture, and as such, you will appear very appetizing. You will look like a gourmet meal, and they will salivate with the potential and opportunity you provide. If you are competent and extremely skilled, they will look at you as a fresh meal in an open desert. Please stay away from teammates who are Absolute Incompetents.

Shark No. 8 – The Hooded Racist

A few years ago, I was shopping at a local farmer's market. It was a beautiful day, and the market was packed. There were no parking spaces. I eventually found a space, but there were two little kids standing in the space. I got out of my car and asked the children to move. I remember being a little concerned that they were standing directly in the space. When the children moved, I parked my car and started inside. Immediately, I was approached by an irate woman who started screaming at me. Through the various profanities and racist language, she stated that I had tried to run over her children. She stated that she had placed her children in the space to save it for her. I was speechless, overwhelmed, and a little perplexed. Who in the heck has children use their bodies to save a parking space? She continued screaming. The market was packed, and not only was she screaming, but also people had gathered to watch. At this point, she told me she was calling the police for my obvious attempt to run over her children.

I was still speechless. The police showed up, and I explained that I had asked her children to move, and her children confirmed my concern for them. The policeman told the woman not to use her children to save a parking space and left. I was so embarrassed. I had said nothing. I felt like the air had been knocked out of me. I do not know if it were a reaction to the parking incident as a child, but I felt so helpless, so lost. I had received a verbal racist beating, and I had done nothing. I had just stood there. Not only was I embarrassed, but also part of me was ashamed. What I did not know was that this was the best reaction I could have: Do nothing. As I walked through the market to buy the items I had come for, many people approached me to see if I were all right. Several people stated that her (the screaming woman's) behavior was so out of line. In other words, I had no reason to be ashamed. I had done everything correctly.

I call this shark the Hooded Racist. These are the sharks that do things in public that you can only imagine. They are the overt racists. You see their behavior captured and placed on social media. Every now and then, they will be a topic in the news or on a television show. Whether they are having a bad day, stressed, or simply extreme racists, they are individuals who will say something that is so out of line that you are awestruck and unsure how to react. I think if I had been younger, I would have responded in kind. I would have yelled back, corrected, called her a racist, told her I did not run over her children. I would have tried to shift the blame to her placing her children in danger. But I did not. Because I did not respond, I learned a very important lesson.

The world has changed since I was seven years old, and the Hooded Racist is no longer tolerated. You do not need to respond if this person confronts you in private or in public. Their inability to understand that their behavior is no longer considered acceptable is their issue.

Unfortunately, I had to learn this lesson again. When I was in grad school, there was a fellow student who would come up to me and publicly say things. The statements he made were sexist, racist, etc. The interesting part was that the professors thought nothing of it, even when he said it in class. At first, I tried to correct him. This made it worse. According to the professors and students, I was the one being difficult. This continued throughout the semester, and I was at a loss. Then I remembered the incident in the parking lot and decided to simply ignore him but with one caveat. I wrote a letter to the president of the university asking why such behavior was tolerated at such a prestigious institution. I said in the letter that my daughter's school (she was in a private elementary school) had a policy as to how students would treat one another and the atmosphere in the classroom. How was it possible for an elementary school to insist on a humane environment for its students and this institution allowed sexist, racists remarks, not only by students, but by professors as well? The president of the university responded. A statement was read in to all students in the program that certain behavior would no longer be tolerated.

You rarely find the Hooded Racist in the office. Most of the time they are found in those off situations. It may be at the supermarket, the bank, or perhaps just as you are standing in line for the latest smart phone. But it will be like an unexpected stomach punch when they let it into you. I know this book is about behavior at the office, but you need to understand that this behavior could happen anywhere, and I want to give you permission to do nothing. Allow the individuals around you to protect you. Allow humanity to come to light and take care of you. Trust in the fact that this is a very rare animal in the jungle, and understand that they are in a world of their own pain. Even if you did yell back and try to educate them (through the anger), it is far better to watch them flap their wings in vain.

Characteristics:

These sharks are of any age, gender, or management level. Basically, they are racists that have anger issues, or something in their life has occurred that they cannot reconcile. They must take it out on someone, and it usually is the weakest in society. They view the weakest as individuals of color or the sales clerk, the maid, or whoever else they deem vulnerable for their wrath.

What they will do to you:

The Hooded Racist will scream at you, normally in public, and without warning. If it is in the office place, it will be a random moment, in which you intersect with someone who is so angry, and you are simply the outlet.

How to recognize:

This is an easy one; it will be like a punch in the stomach. The statements this person makes will be vile. They will scream, yell, and terrorize you. There are times when they will quietly speak so no one can hear them, but the result will still be the same. You will be so put off that part of you will want to respond.

Survival Guide for the Hooded Racist:

- When you are confronted with a Hooded Racist, your first goal is to ensure your safety. If the confrontation is in public, you should be okay. However, if it is in private, it is important that you go to a public place and find safety as soon as possible. Go to a public place and leave the situation immediately.

- Do not respond. Do not tell them to be quiet. Do not try to defend yourself from the verbal abuse. If you are in public, stand there and slowly walk away. If you are in private, as stated above, find a safe place as soon as possible. One of the nice evolutions of our world is that there is far less racism than there was fifty years ago. In a crowd, you will find that there will be people who will support you and protect you. Much like my experience at the market, I learned that by standing there and allowing the woman to vent, I was protected, and I had placed myself outside of the anger and the fray. If I had responded, I would have been seen just like the woman who was yelling. Whether in the office or standing in line, a Hooded Racist should not be responded to with anger or in kind. Stand back and allow the magnitude and hatred of their act to be publicly identified. Know that this is one time when your inaction is the perfect action. There is no win with the Hooded Racist, but you can make it their loss.

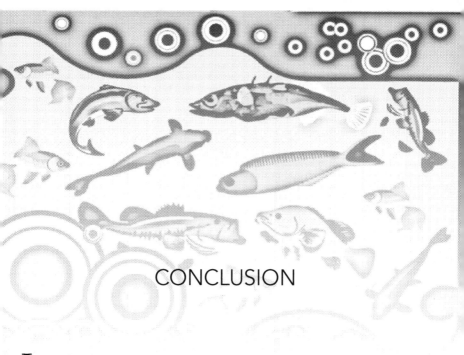

CONCLUSION

In chapter 3, I spoke about my experience of racism in a department store in Atlanta, Georgia. Many years later, I was meeting a client for lunch at a hotel downtown in Washington DC. The was a small boutique hotel, and it had a restaurant with an entrance from the street. I ordered my coffee and started reading the newspaper, awaiting the arrival of my client. After about ten minutes, a homeless black man came in from the street and stood at the entrance. The maître d' approached him and said, "How many in your party, sir?" He said it with such kindness that I am sure if the man had said one, he would have been seated. In my life, I have seen great many acts of kindness, but I have seen few acts of grace. An act of grace is when you extend humanity in such a way that you elevate an individual's perception of themselves. You remind them that they are "of value." Giving is important, but giving with respect is a rare art. It is important to remember that although we experience racism every single day, we also at times experience and can create acts of grace.

When I started working in white corporate America, I went from a naïve employee to an employee who felt devalued. I knew that I had to find a way to create value within my position, from a place of no value. This is the grace within the race. Finding your unique skills or whatever you bring to the world is important. Everyone should seek this. Being able to contribute your skills from a place of value is a blessing. In developing the skills to counter the acts designed to devalue me, to remind me that I am less, I found a way to swim with sharks. It took me twenty years to discover that I could have raced and worked with grace in corporate white America.

My hope is that this book saves you the time, effort, and pain that I went through; that with discipline and courage, you too can swim with sharks in dark water; that you find your unique success, grace, and place in white corporate America.

Printed in the United States
By Bookmasters